Start Your Own

EXECUTIVE RECRUITING SERVICE

Additional titles in *Entrepreneur's* **Startup Series**

Start Your Own

Entrepreneur
MAGAZINE'S

startup

Start Your Own

2ND EDITION

EXECUTIVE RECRUITING SERVICE

Your Step-by-Step Guide to Success

Entrepreneur Press and Courtney Thurman

EP
Entrepreneur
Press

Editorial Director: Jere L. Calmes
Managing Editor: Marla Markman
Cover Design: Beth Hansen-Winter
Production and Composition: Eliot House Productions

This publication is designed to provide accurate and authoritative information in regard to the subject matter covered. It is sold with the understanding that the publisher is not engaged in rendering legal, accounting or other professional services. If legal advice or other expert assistance is required, the services of a competent professional person should be sought.

Quick quote icon: ©Georgios Kollidas

Library of Congress Cataloging-in-Publication Data

Thurman, Courtney.
  Start your own executive recruiting business/by Entrepreneur Press and Courtney Thurman—2nd ed.
     p.   cm.
  Rev. ed. of: Start your own executive recruiting service/Mandy Erickson. ©2003.
  Includes index.
  ISBN-13: 978-1-59918-126-4 (alk. paper)
  ISBN-10: 1-59918-126-6 (alk. paper)
     1. Executive search firms. 2. Executives—Recruiting. 3. Executive search firms—Management. 4. New business enterprises—Management. I. Thurman, Courtney. II. Erickson, Mandy. Start your own executive recruiting service. III. Entrepreneur Press.
  HF5549.5.R44E75 2007
  658.4'071110681—dc22   2007023254

Printed in Canada

12 11 10 09 08 07   10 9 8 7 6 5 4 3 2 1

Contents

Preface

Seventy phone calls a day. If your phone is already permanently fixed to your ear, this may be the industry for you.

Executive recruiters typically spend at least four solid hours on the phone; some people will be willing to talk to you, and many won't. But it takes just a few cases where the match is made that can get a recruiter addicted to what they do and absolutely love doing it.

Does it sound like that could be you? It takes a certain personality type to survive in the recruiting world: extroverted, tenacious, and thick-skinned. You must love yakking on the phone, never bat an eye at making cold calls, and welcome rejection as part of the job. You also need to be attentive to detail, patient, and good at negotiating a deal. The business is people-based so if you have the people skills, you have picked up the right book.

Maybe you are checking out this book after hearing about the growth in the industry and you want to get into it yourself for the first time. Or maybe you're currently working in the industry and you want to start a business with your own clients.

If this describes you, read on. Executive recruiting can be quite rewarding and lucrative, with salaries as high as six or even seven figures. It's also very competitive: Three-quarters of recruiting firms fail within the first few years.

Read this book carefully and be honest with yourself about your abilities—then you'll be a good judge of whether starting a recruiting business will be a good investment of your time. And if you decide it is, this book will help you become one of the success stories. We will give you an overview of the business and provide resources in the Appendix to do your specialized research. It takes a lot of research to start up a business, but with this book, you will have a roadmap.

In the following pages you'll learn about the experience and training you need before you can start your own business. Taking a job with a recruiting firm or purchasing a franchise that offers training is usually the best way to go.

When you're ready, this book will help you hang out a shingle, including choosing a specialty, finding clients, developing contacts, and building a reputation. You'll discover the different ways recruiters work—on contingency or retained by a client—and find which approach may work best for you. You'll also learn what recruiters charge for their services, when they bill, and how to draw up a contract.

This book will walk you through the steps of recruiting candidates for a position, from gathering resumes, interviewing, and making background checks to presenting the top candidates to your client.

You'll learn how to weather a recession, how to maintain good relations with your clients, and how to keep up with the news in your specialty.

Because your business may grow enough that you may need help finding candidates for jobs, this book covers hiring, managing, and training employees. It also discusses when it helps to have recruiters working for you and when it makes more sense to go it alone.

Finally, you'll learn how to evaluate your performance to find your weak areas and become a more effective, and better paid, recruiter.

As comprehensive as this book is, it can't tell you everything you need to know to start up a recruiting business. A lot depends on your connections, your chosen specialty, your location, and the state of the economy. There are so many facets to this business that you will need to do additional targeted research into your specialty. This book will help point you in the right direction. An appendix full of resources—including consultants, associations, newsletters, and books—will help you find answers to your questions.

Starting up a recruiting business is a big commitment of time and energy. You want to weigh your decisions as carefully as possible, consider all the options, and be aware of potential downfalls. This book will help you do just that.

1

Recruiting
Realities

Agood analogy when looking at this industry might be that when employees change jobs they become professionally single and are looking to get back into the employment dating scene. The search begins and so can the excitement of finding the perfect match. The arrangement needs to work for both parties.

Given how frequently employees change jobs, it should come as no surprise that executive recruiters, also commonly known as headhunters, are rapidly increasing in numbers. The more people change jobs, the more work there is for recruiters, and the more matches to be made. Unfortunately, this business is also terribly competitive for that reason.

In this chapter we'll give you an idea of what the executive recruiting business is all about. We'll start with an overview of the industry, including how much money a recruiter can hope to make and what the competition is like. We'll also look back at how this business got started and take a peek into the future.

Recruiting 101

In a nutshell, a recruiter is someone who is hired by a company to find people qualified to fill a job opening—candidates. Often, companies hire recruiters only after they've tried to fill the positions themselves. Recruiters usually work on a project-by-project basis. The client company pays the recruiter a percentage—between 20 and 35 percent—of the annual salary of the candidate who accepts the position. While the recruiter finds and screens candidates for the job, the client company makes the final decision on which person to hire.

Recruiting is an unregulated business, so industry statistics are difficult to come by, but Paul Hawkinson, publisher of *The Fordyce Letter*, puts recruiting at a $10 billion—and growing—industry. There are about 5,000 recruiting firms in the United States, he says. A few very large firms dominate the industry, but most are very small: The average-size recruiting company has between two and three people.

One common assumption about the industry is that it's just a matching business between employer and potential employee. Being a recruiter isn't as much about finding candidates as much as it's a sales job. You have to sell yourself to the client to get the job assignment before you can go looking for candidates. "This is a sales job, no matter how you cut it," says Hawkinson.

Actually, there are three separate sales that need to be made before you earn any money as a recruiter. First, you need to sell the company on your ability to fill the open position, then sell the candidates on interviewing for the opening, and finally, sell the company on the candidates that you present. There are numerous recruiters are out there competing for these jobs and candidates, which is why

> **Bright Idea**
>
> Paul Hawkinson, editor of *The Fordyce Letter*, has written an excellent article titled, "So You Want to Be an Executive Recruiter," which is available online. Visit www.fordyceletter.com to order this article. Click on the Special Reports link.

many experts estimate the dropout rate within the first year is between 80 and 90 percent.

Contingency vs. Retained

Recruiters generally work in one of two ways: contingency or retained. If a recruiter works on contingency, it means they take an assignment on spec—a client asks them to fill an open position, but will pay them only if they find the candidate who eventually accepts the job. For recruiters who work on retainer, the client pays the recruiter before they start the search. A retained recruiter pretty much has to guarantee that he or she will fill the client's position. Between two-thirds and three-quarters of the recruiters in the United States work on contingency. The rest are retained or a combination of retained and contingency.

Working on retainer is generally viewed as the more prestigious billing method, and client companies generally retain recruiters for filling those positions at the top of the corporate ladder. Contingency recruiting is the domain of new recruiters and those who place lower-level employees.

"The retained recruiters are considered the silk slipper people of the industry," says Paul Hawkinson, editor and publisher of *The Fordyce Letter*, a newsletter for recruiters, "to the extent that they generally work these higher-level openings, and they're dealing with CEOs and presidents and CFOs."

A contingency job means you don't get a dime until you place a candidate with a client. With contingency jobs, you will often be competing with other recruiters trying to fill the same position. Because contingency recruiters fill only a fraction of the positions they're trying to fill, they will work on as many as 30 or 40 jobs at a time.

A retained assignment means the client pays you up front to start a search, usually in installments. With retainer jobs, also known as exclusives, you will be the only recruiter. Unlike contingency recruiters, retained recruiters work on just a few jobs at a time.

Some clients like to hire on a retained basis. Because the recruiter is paid up front, the client knows that the recruiter is less concerned with simply filling the position (so he or she will get paid) than with finding appropriate candidates. Also, because retained recruiters work on fewer assignments at a time, they can focus more of their efforts on each assignment, conducting more extensive background and reference checks than contingency recruiters.

Other clients prefer to use a contingency approach. This strategy lets them use several recruiters, who will bring in more candidates for the position than one recruiter will. Or the company may be doing its own recruiting, and if it succeeds in hiring someone, it won't have to pay a recruiter. Also, a company may want to use a contingency approach to try out a new recruiter.

Quick Quote

Entrepreneur Mark M. estimates that "Approximately 90 percent of executive recruiting companies are boutique firms."

While some clients always prefer to go with big name recruiting companies, many others use smaller firms because of the usual advantages small businesses offer—more personal service and often a lower price. Also, the big firms generally use the retained payment structure, so clients who want contingency recruiters will use smaller firms.

Recruiters tend to specialize in one industry, such as electrical engineering, finance, or law enforcement. Doing so allows them to understand one industry and the players in that industry thoroughly.

Why Use a Recruiter?

Recruiting is essentially a consulting business. A company doesn't have to hire a recruiter, just as it doesn't have to hire a management consultant; but a recruiter, like a consultant, can save the company time and money.

Executive recruiting entrepreneur Jeff H. of Chesterfield, Missouri, now runs his own executive recruiting group and also leads a few industry associations. "As a [former] foodservice executive, I never wanted to spend money with a recruiter, but we all want the best talent. Smart hires make us money and the better the talent, the more money we can put on the bottom line. With this in mind, recruiting fees are reasonably insignificant in the scope of a management employee's term of employment. A good manager can make a company hundreds of thousands of dollars and as we all know, a bad manager can cost you that or more in a short period of time."

Recruiters take over the job many managers don't have time for—finding and screening candidates for a job. But more important, recruiters can find candidates quickly. They usually know so many people in their area of expertise that they can pick up the phone, ask who might be interested, and within a week or so get a list of names.

Recruiters also find quality candidates—again, they have so many contacts they'll hear about the bad seeds that might interview well but have performance shortfalls. Conversely, they can refer candidates who don't sell themselves well but make exceptional employees.

Jeff H. explains that "Roughly 5 percent of the workforce consists of unemployed workers who are actively looking for jobs, networking, answering ads, etc. You don't necessarily need recruiters to find these candidates. Some 35 percent of the workforce is not happy with their current employment for various reasons, from nonperformance pressure, company instability, career ceiling, etc. You don't necessarily need recruiters to find these candidates because they are also actively networking, answering ads, and using recruiters."

He continues, "But, what most people seem to forget is that roughly 60 percent of the workforce is happy with their current position, earning bonuses, being promoted, and very well thought of by their companies. These people are not networking, answering ads, or even considering leaving their current employer. These are the best candidates, and you will only find them with the assistance of a qualified professional recruiter."

Recruiters provide an unbiased assessment of the candidates for the job. A manager's opinion is often colored by the fact that a candidate attended the same school or enjoys the same hobbies, causing him or her to overlook the fact that the candidate has never managed a staff or made a sale.

Besides providing qualified candidates quickly, a recruiter can help a company throughout the hiring process. A recruiter can advise what salary the company can expect to pay its hires, how to better interview candidates, and how to negotiate hiring conditions. In short, a recruiter can act as a hiring consultant to companies.

Jeff H. says that, "The best recruiters can actually save a company money, by managing the process efficiently. Too often companies hire reduced-fee contingency recruiters who send them 15 or 20 resumes, of which the company interviews five candidates and many times hire none. A good recruiter will provide three or four candidates. You can pick the one or two best and hire one, saving substantial dollars in travel and other related interview costs, not to mention time. The rate of the fee is by no means a company's true cost."

It's a Dog-Eat-Dog Business

One reason so many people try to get into recruiting is that the business can be exceptionally lucrative. Some recruiting entrepreneurs make as much as $3 to $4 million a year. Before your eyes drop out of their sockets, be aware that these people are very much the exception. The average recruiter makes between $100,000 and $125,000 a year. Not a bad salary, certainly, but keep in mind that there are also many who make $30,000 a year or less (it takes an awful lot of low earners to balance out those millionaires).

Another reason that people are attracted to the recruiting industry is that it requires no exams, no degrees, and very little money to get started. The industry is

▲

unregulated, so literally anyone can give the business a shot. Other than being knowledgeable about a particular field and having contacts in that field, all you really need to do the job is a minimal amount of equipment—likely what you already have at home.

"There are no barriers to entry for the executive search business," says Joseph Daniel McCool, editor of *Executive Recruiter News*, a newsletter for recruiters who work on a retained basis. "If someone wants to be successful in executive recruiting, they need only have a solid background in a particular industry, an incredible network of professional contacts, and people skills. Other than that, it's just a telephone and some business cards."

So we have a business that has the potential to make you a millionaire and that costs you almost nothing to get started. What does this mean? Competition—and lots of it. There are thousands of people out there with the same idea. They're thinking "It's nearly cost-free, it could net me a lot of money—why not give it a try?"

Paul Hawkinson, publisher of The Fordyce Letter says that being a recruiter takes a "high tolerance for rejection, and true grit." Recruiters must make sales calls seeking assignments with client companies, while simultaneously finding candidates to fill the openings. They are paid either straight commissions or a periodic "draw," an amount deducted from future revenues they'll generate.

As a result, McCool estimates that 75 to 80 percent of recruiting firms fail within five years. Most recruiters who take a job with an existing firm also leave within two years.

Casting a Net

A recruiter's job is all about networking and finding information, so it should come as no surprise that online accessibility has radically changed the way recruiters do their business in the past ten years. Recruiters can often find candidates by going to company web sites that compete with their client companies and checking out job listing sites, visiting newsgroups where people with certain skills hang out, and using search engines to locate names, organizations, and even zip codes. Prior to all this information being available online, they had to find what information they could by phone—a time-consuming and sometimes fruitless process.

Naturally, e-mails to and from clients and job candidates speeds up the process once the candidates are located, too. But recruiters warn that as convenient as working remotely is, they still need to do old-fashioned networking and phone calling. Nothing works like the personal touch.

Stat Fact

The Association of Executive Search Consultants (AESC) reported a record year for executive search revenues with over a 17 percent increase from 2005 to 2006, showing a third consecutive year of industry growth. Check out their current reports at www.aesc.org.

Who Are the Players?

Like with other industries, there are big players here too. We covered the difference between contingency and retained executive recruiters, and the biggest contingent recruiting company is Robert Half, which is also publicly-traded. They tend to do hiring for positions up to $100K.

The big retained executive recruiting companies are the ones that go for positions that pay $200K or higher. The top four players in this field are Heidrich & Struggles, Korn Ferry, Spencer Stuart, and Russel Reynolds. For your research, check out their web sites for industry and background information.

Now a lot of executive recruiting entrepreneurs are looking for a blend of contingency and retainer methods, which would be called "container" or "retingency" recruiting. This type is usually for positions between $75K–$150K. The deal is that the company pays one third upfront, another third when they present the candidates, and the last third when they are finally placed. This is a performance-based way to get in the door.

Each industry or position has their share of recruiting companies competing within it. Do your research to find your competition and check out their web sites. It's important to see who the players are in your specialized arena.

How the Industry Began

It's a good bet that throughout history, whenever there were worker shortages, some form of recruiting helped fill the bill. But the first record of an employment service was in 14th century Germany. The first record in the United States was an employment exchange in Boston in 1848.

The first modern-style retained search firm was started in 1926 by Thorndike Deland, who concentrated on placing people in the retail industry. Larger consulting firms got into the act and started adding candidate searches to their consulting practices.

Quick Quote

"Knowledge is power only if a man knows what facts not to bother about."

—Robert Lynd, excerpted from *The Fordyce Letter*

There were many other placement agencies, but the approach was completely different from what it is now—job applicants, not employers, had to pay fees to get the firms to place them in positions. That changed in the late '50s, with the advent of the defense and chemical processing industries, according to Hawkinson. These businesses had big government support, so they could pass costs onto the Feds.

Stat Fact
According to the U.S. Bureau of Labor Statistics, the management consulting industry, which includes executive recruiting, is the third fastest-growing industry based on the rate of change projected from 2004 to 2014.

"They needed a lot of people and they needed them quickly, and they couldn't find them through ads, so they went to recruiters. The recruiters said 'You need to pay a fee.' That's when companies got used to paying a fee for their services," says Hawkinson.

Then other businesses found out that "recruiters are more effective than alternative methods, paying a fee is tax-deductible and a good investment, and most applicants are unwilling to pay a fee to find a job," Hawkinson adds. The industry grew during the '60s, but dipped during the '70s, he says. "The '70s weren't bad, but the recessions came and went, and you lost a lot of practitioners during the down times. When the boom times came again, they got back into it."

Those boom times were the '90s, when some search firms went public and the media discovered them. "The 1990s were really the golden age of executive search," says McCool. Worker shortages in the late '90s and early '00s caused many more businesses to turn to executive search, and more and more recruiters got into the business.

Looking at Industry Growth

Stat Fact
The U.S. Bureau of Labor Statistics estimates that 78 million people are considered Baby Boomers. Given that Generation X includes only 49 million people, the future employment shortage is clear.

There's no end in sight for boom times in recruiting. The industry has doubled every five years, and it continues to do so. More businesses, even smaller companies that typically don't use recruiters, are turning to search firms to fill their open slots. They're recognizing the value recruiters can offer them, and they're willing to pay their fees.

Whether the economy slows or not, executive search will become even more critical as baby boomers retire, McCool points out. Companies turn to recruiters not because they have money to burn, but because they're having

> **Fun Fact**
>
> Recruiters noticed a trend shift in 2006 that it became a candidate-driven market. Candidates sometimes had several offers and could be highly selective which caused the clients to reevaluate their compensation packages to capture quality candidates.

trouble filling positions. "Corporations are going to be faced with some really monumental tasks, and search firms will be well-positioned to assist them," McCool says.

Entrepreneur Mark M. says that "The industry has a seven-year cycle between candidate and client-driven markets. The next several years will be candidate-driven because of the higher salaries that will be offered and the abundance of hiring companies. The need for recruiters will abound since employers will want employed managers who are not looking for a job."

Mark M. says that everyone looking at getting into the industry is picking a great time. "Unemployment is at a five-year low, and the baby boomers are retiring—do the math. It is a fantastic time, the best ever to be a recruiter. The economy is growing and globalizing. We live in the 'information age' where workers need specialized skills. These folks will be more in demand than ever."

He forecasts that, "The next five to six years are going to be the best for recruiters because of the retiring baby boomers which will open many senior management positions and the job orders will be abundant. It's a booming economy and there will be a war for qualified talent."

Now that you have a roadmap of the recruiting industry, we're going to look at whether it's the right business for you.

What It Takes
to Succeed

Now that we've filled you in on the basics of the industry, it's time to see whether it's the right one for you. Do you have the experience to start a recruiting business? Do you have the money? Most of all, do you have the right personality? It's easy to get into the recruiting business, but it's difficult to stick with it. An honest assessment of your skills and capabilities will help you know if starting a recruiting business will be a good game plan for you.

Is It in You?

Many experts have written about the characteristics necessary to be a great recruiter and most of them agree on the similarities they've seen in top billers. Check out the Self-Assessment Worksheet on page 14.

- *Edgy and hungry.* Although there are a lot of interpersonal soft skills that go into being a great recruiter, at their core, successful recruiters are edgy and will do what it takes to make a placement. They don't let anyone else tred on their territory and are skeptical about a match until it happens. They are cautiously optimistic but always looking at their pipeline too. They are never satisfied with just making enough placements to fill a quota or only making a comfortable income. When they aren't at their peak, they start getting irritable and refuse to be distracted.

- *Flexible in the face of adversity.* Each recruiter picks their own specialties, but it's those who adapt to changes, overcome obstacles or rebounded from failure that tend to be resilient enough to adapt to the ebb and flow of the industry. This is character-specific and it can't be taught.

- *Savvy and keen.* The successful ones tend to have a savvy way that comes from experience, not from education. They understand what it means to work to a goal instead of being handed an opportunity. This is a people business and it takes intuition and experience to get to the top.

- *Applicable experience.* Many experts say that you may not have been a recruiter before, but those who succeed came from a similar experience that may not look like a sales job but gave them the skills they needed. Not all sales jobs are the same and there are other jobs that teach more sales skills than a sales job would. Convincing someone to do anything or learn something that they may not have wanted to otherwise is more of a sale than working in retail.

- *A history of tenacity.* What's your track record? Have you routinely overcome odds and achieved your goals even if you didn't have an advantage? If in your

personal and professional experience you've overcome obstacles and consistently muscle through the learning curve, this may be a good fit for you. If you aren't ready to put in the effort or are looking for a get-rich-quick job, this isn't the industry for you.

- *Seeing green.* If you aren't sitting on a trust fund, need or want a large income, and are willing to do the hard work and training necessary to get it, you are running with the same pack as the other successful recruiters out there. Those who are money and success-driven tend to have the hunger that's needed to plow through those cold calls.

> **Fun Fact**
>
> AESC, the Association of Executive Search Consultants did a recent poll asking recruiters what characteristics were most critical for success. The top responses were: communication skills, interpersonal skills, and integrity.

- *Competitive and determined.* Are we seeing a theme? If you've always been competitive, and the idea of another recruiter getting the job order that you want galls you, then you might be putting yourself in the right race. This industry has the capacity to make you rich, but you have to beat out the other recruiters to get those placements. Use the Personal Goals Worksheet on page 16.

A Taste for Recruiting

Working for another recruiting firm will help you gain valuable experience you can apply to your own business. But there's a better reason to work for someone else before striking out on your own. You'll want to know if you can stomach the job. At least half the recruiters who take jobs with firms leave the business within two years.

> **Fun Fact**
>
> Think you're ready to start a business? Do you know your EQ (Entrepreneurial Quotient)? Many entrepreneurs have common characteristics and they have a running trend in entrepreneurial studies. Take the quiz in *Entrepreneur Magazine's Start Your Own Business* to see how you score.

Ken C., an experienced recruiter and the founder of the National Association of Executive Recruiters, says that many people new to recruiting think they can do the job because they know how to find candidates. They don't realize how hard it is to find clients.

"That's a mistake an awful lot of people make. They think 'Well, I'm good at finding

Self-Assessment Worksheet

Use this self-assessment worksheet to see if working for yourself is right for you. After you've completed all the questions, look for a pattern in the answers. For example, do you see a need for your services and skills in areas where you excel?

○ List at least five things you like to do or excel in at work:

1. _____
2. _____
3. _____
4. _____
5. _____

○ List at least five things you don't like or areas where you need to improve at work:

1. _____
2. _____
3. _____
4. _____
5. _____

○ List three services that would make your life easier at work:

1. _____
2. _____
3. _____

○ When people ask you what you do, what's your answer? _____

_____

○ List three things you enjoy about your work:

1. _____
2. _____
3. _____

Self-Assessment Worksheet, continued

○ List three things you dislike about your work:

    1. _____

    2. _____

    3. _____

○ When people tell you what they like most about you, they say: _____

_____

○ Some people dislike the fact that you: _____

_____

○ Other than your main occupation, list any other skills you possess, whether you excel at them or not: _____

_____

_____

○ In addition to becoming more financially independent, you would also like to become more: _____

_____

_____

○ List at least three things you would like to improve about your personal life:

    1. _____

    2. _____

    3. _____

○ List three things you think need to be improved in your industry:

    1. _____

    2. _____

    3. _____

Adapted from *Entrepreneur* Magazine's *Start Your Own Business*.

Personal Goals Worksheet

To accomplish professional or personal goals, you need to lay out a roadmap for your-self. Come back to this worksheet on a regular basis since your goals may change and you will want to track your progress.

○ Being an entrepreneur is important to me because: _____

_____

○ What I like best about the idea of working for myself is: _____

_____

○ In five years, I would like my business to be: _____

_____

_____

○ When I look back over the past five years of my career, I feel: _____

_____

_____

○ My financial situation now is: _____

_____

○ The most important part of my business will be: _____

_____

○ The area of my business I know I will really need to excel in is: _____

_____

Adapted from *Entrepreneur* Magazine's *Start Your Own Business.*

Bright Idea

For a fun way to get to know yourself a little bit better, try doing a personality test such as the Meyers-Briggs indicator. You can find these types of tests at your local career center or library. You can also try doing a search online using the keywords "Meyers-Briggs." One web site to check out for Meyers-Briggs and other personality tests is www.keirsey.com.

people, so I'll be good at being a headhunter.' Like all consulting, the hardest part is getting someone to pay you. A lot of people manage to starve themselves to death because they're not good at getting someone to pay them."

Hawkinson agrees that drumming up business is by far the most difficult part of the job. "You're on the phone with 50 or 60 potential clients a day, trying to persuade them to do business with you, to give you a job opening and pay your fee. Forty-nine to 55 of them are going to say no, and if you're not up for the rejection, this can be a brutal business."

He adds that recruiters must be good salespeople. "This is a sales job, pure and simple," Hawkinson says. "People like to call themselves consultants, they like to call themselves counselors, they like to call themselves account execs and all kinds of other highfalutin titles, but the main fact is you're a salesperson. You're selling a company on using your services; you're selling a candidate on taking a look at the opportunities your clients present. You're selling all the time. You have to be a persuader and a negotiator."

Larry D. agrees: "It's almost a requirement that you have a selling background," he says. "If you've never sold before, it's a very, very difficult transition. The vast majority of people who are successful in this are people who've sold."

So if you don't blink when you hear the word "No," and you're confident of your sales abilities, you are on the right path. But what sort of personality is suited to recruiting? In a word, "extroverts." Recruiters spend all day—and sometimes all evening—talking to people. They must keep in touch with hundreds of contacts on a regular basis. The more people they know, the better they'll do.

"I've made so many placements and so many clients through my friends," says Tamara L. "Everybody I know is a potential client or potential candidate, or a referring client or a referring candidate."

Recruiting is definitely not for everybody. "You either love it or hate it," says Donna K. "The good thing is, you'll know early on."

Smart Tip

Successful recruiters are the ones who take the attitude that they're acting as a consultant to the client, not just filling vacancies. Clients will quickly see through someone who doesn't have their interests at heart.

Experience Highly Recommended

Most of the entrepreneurs interviewed for this book gained experience before they opened their own businesses. They worked for other recruiters or as recruiters in large companies, learned the basics, built up a network of contacts, then applied what they learned to their own firms.

The feedback we received is that although some recruiters have gotten into the industry without experience, those individuals are at a disadvantage compared to others who have worked for a recruiting firm or been an in-house hiring manager.

Donna K., who runs her own firm in New York City, says that she worked for a small recruiting firm for three years before striking out on her own. Her supervisor taught her the ins and outs of the business, but she found that the arrangement she had with her boss prevented her from growing professionally. Her boss handled all jobs more than $50,000 a year, and she handled all those less than $50,000. So the candidates she placed were out of her reach once they started earning more money. "After about three years, they were outgrowing me," she said. "It was frustrating that I was giving up a lot of the relationships that I had worked so hard to gain."

Tamara L., who opened a firm in San Mateo, California, is another entrepreneur who opened her own shop after leaving a recruiting firm. Her boss taught her the skills she needed to succeed, but eventually, she said, "I wanted to have my own ownership. There was a lot we could have been doing better."

Neither Manny A. in Chicago, nor Ken C. in Panama City Beach, Florida, had worked for recruiting firms before they started their own businesses. But they performed recruiting functions within large companies. Manny found that he wanted to be in business for himself. Ken was laid off from his job when he decided to start his own recruiting business. "I said to myself, 'This is never going to happen to you again,'" remembers Ken. "I knew I was a good recruiter, and I was pretty sure that people would pay me to locate people for them."

There's a process—and an art—to signing on clients, finding candidates, approaching them about job opportunities, and selling them to employers. While you can learn some of the techniques through reading or even taking human resource courses in a college, practical experience is invaluable. Working for another firm will let you practice those skills. Also, being able to point to your own experience will make it easier for you to sell your services to clients.

"If you try to start an executive search firm without any human resource or recruitment experience, then it's going to be a very difficult mountain to climb," says McCool of Executive Recruiter News. "There's really nothing like the practical experience."

Mark M. had experience with the largest contingent recruiting firm, Robert Half International, but still says that it was hard launching his own business. "I took to 'headhunting' like a duck to water and have been a recruiter for 12 years now. Like many good recruiters I started my company because I felt I could do it better and more happily 'on my own.' Little did I realize the difficulty and that is it MUCH more than just doing the job of a recruiter. You have to incorporate, write a comprehensive business plan, worry about systems, buying lists, finding a lawyer, and getting the right insurance in place! You also MUST be well-capitalized and have access to funds to tide you over until you bring in that first check (could be three or four months!) Working as a solo is tough, and if you are used to having comrades and teammates, it can be unbearable."

Recruiters agree that the best way is to get a job, even for a few years, at a recruiting firm or in the human resources department of a large company. Some people do try to start recruiting firms without practical experience, as no degrees or certificates are required and very little money is needed to start. But if you decide to give it a go without working in the business first, be aware that your chances of succeeding are slim.

Get Yourself Trained and Certified

Anything worth doing takes time and effort and throwing some energy towards training is always a good idea. Jeff H. strongly recommends getting certified as a Certified Personnel Consultant (CPC). "The CPC certification is for the recruiting industry as the CPA is for accountants. There are continuing education requirements and an intense exam covering everything regarding legal, ethical, and technical issues. The top recruiting professionals have cared enough about their industry and taken the time to earn a CPC."

One trend in the industry is that certification programs are becoming more popular to raise the bar for quality and ethics. A common certification is the AIRS Certification which emphasizes continuing education and professional development. Information about this certification can be found on their web site at www.airs.org.

More organizations are focusing on certification, and an Association of Executive Search Consultants (AESC) Member Firm, Boyden World Corporation, just released that they will also be launching an Executive Recruiter Certification Program as well. Their program would "require all new associates to complete an intensive curriculum of online courses in

Smart Tip

Tip...

If you want to get a better feel for the recruiting industry, attend the annual conference of the National Association of Personnel Services—the largest organization that covers recruiters of all stripes (see the Appendix for contact information).

candidate assessment, techniques, background and reference checking, search methodology and candidate development."

Jeff H. says that he wishes "that all recruiting entrepreneurs would learn to do business properly and to improve the professionalism of the overall industry. He advocates for certification and recommends getting a mentor to show them the ropes. If you are going to get training, go to the best. Get the best training available."

3

What Is the Day-to-Day?

Executive recruiters have a lot of work on their hands when they get a job to fill for a client, and that means long days and oftentimes weekends too. So what does the day-to-day look like at a glance? In this chapter, we will discuss cold call requirements, the steps most recruiters take to fill a position, and what a typical day might look like for you.

Can You Do the Work?

Quick Quote

"Our business is unique. I know of no other business where the players start with nothing to sell, no one to sell it to, and wind up at the end with a five-figure fee for doing it."

—Paul Hawkinson,
The Fordyce Letter

Executive recruiting is not for the faint of heart. Cold-calling is a necessity and if you think that you can make a cushy living by surfing the internet without picking up the phone then this book has already saved you a costly wake-up call.

Cold-calling is hard. It's not just picking up the phone, dialing and reading off a script. It is just one part of the puzzle. First you have to know where to look, who to talk to (or who not to), and overcome obstacles to even connect with a potential candidate, and then they may not be open to looking at a new job or know anyone who is. Like we said above, it takes street smarts to navigate the candidate market to find those fresh candidates.

You need skills to do the right research, networking, and cold-calling. Just because the technology and online job boards are so advanced doesn't mean that there isn't true skill required to find the candidates you need.

Executive recruiter Mark M. says that the industry has changed but has stayed very much the same. "The tools have changed somewhat just in the 12 years I have been a headhunter, such as computers, the internet, fancy databases, cell phones, etc. However the core business of recruiting; the core foundation is people talking to one another. This is a "contact sport" and quite simply the more people you talk to (clients and candidates) the more money you make."

There are basically two kinds of recruiters, just like there are two kinds of candidates—active and passive. Passive recruiters partner with actively seeking candidates, the ones that are actively pursuing jobs online and have the stigma of being less appealing as a potential hires. Remember, these are the candidates that the client could find themselves; they hired you to find the passive candidates that aren't showcasing their availability.

Active recruiters are looking for those passive candidates that aren't putting their resumes online or searching for a new job but would be interested if given the right opportunity. Those passive candidates are the ones that fill positions best, usually because the assumption is that they are excelling in their current jobs. Not that an active candidate couldn't be a good candidate, but they are the "low hanging fruit" that the passive recruiters could find.

The difference between active and passive recruiters is summarized by many experts by these three characteristics:

1. *Dedication*. If you run out of names from your resume inventory or your job board membership, what do you do? You pick up the phone and get to cold-calling.

The candidates are out there and it takes true commitment to find them. It is simply the best way to network with new people, develop new business and make a lot of money.

2. *Creativity*. What sets you apart from the next recruiter? You want to make that placement and you will have to be resourceful. Recruiters that solely rely on keywords on job boards aren't going to get as many names as those who cold-call, get references, back-door entry to names or cross-reference. How can you find someone that won't be on a job board?

3. *Tenacity*. Why do successful recruiters make so much money? They outlasted most of the other people that started at the same time and are succeeding because they have the capacity to be unfazed by the rejection from cold-calls. There's going to be a lot of bad calls and disappointment before there are the big bucks, but if you can stomach it, you are doing better than most.

Obviously, if you're the type to cringe when the phone rings, or if your idea of a perfect day is taking a long hike by yourself, this is not the business for you.

Here are some other traits you need to be a good recruiter:

- *Attention to detail*. You'll need to keep track of all those potential clients and possible candidates—when you called last, how many phone messages you left, and when they're available to talk.

- *Negotiating skills*. To broker a deal between a candidate and a client, you'll need the diplomacy and creativity to see the deal to its conclusion.

- *The ability to listen and observe*. You must be able to read your clients on what they want in a candidate and your candidates on what they want in an employer. You'll also need to assess candidates well in an interview.

- *Patience*. Clients will change their minds; candidates will back out, and everything will take longer than you had hoped. You'll have to accept these delays and disappointments with a smile.

Executive Recruiting Steps

Executive recruiters have a formula that they follow to make sure they cover their bases. Here are some steps that most recruiters follow, although each recruiter may complete the process a bit differently. Don't miss any steps or you might lose out on a placement.

Mark M. says recruiting is a "complicated math problem. Skip any steps and you get a

> **Quick Quote**
>
> California entrepreneur Mark M. says that "There is success in systems. Recruiters are brokers of information."

different answer than the guy next to you. You can't skip from step 12 to 17. For example, what if you forget to ask the candidate if they are interviewing elsewhere?"

Each recruiter has their own process, but there are many basic steps that need to be taken to facilitate a placement. Below, we have compiled a list of basic steps to complete as an executive recruiter.

Getting the Order

- Get the company information through marketing efforts
- Close on job order with client
- Assess urgency level for the open position
- Complete a candidate profile
- Get position information
- Sign Fee Agreement

Complete a Needs Analysis

- Interview hiring manager for technical priorities
- What results do they expect within the first year?
- Background of the last three successful hires
- Requested companies to target?

Build a Road Map

- Create your strategic recruiting plan
- Where will you get the candidates?
- How will you present the opportunity?
- What will be your main selling points?

Create an Assignment Profile

- Craft the job description
- Build a personality profile
- List the required characteristics for the position

Do Your Research

- Compile a list of source companies
- Submit to client to add or remove companies
- Research industry to locate talent pool
- Check existing databases for leads
- Brainstorm job titles that possess similar characteristics

Search Process

- Begin the search process by hunting for candidates
- Qualify candidates by initial phone interviews
- Prescreen qualified candidates to gauge sincerity
- Conduct indepth in-person interviews with potential finalists
- Consolidate candidate list to finalists

Reference Checkpoint

- Comply with client guidelines for areas of concern or interest
- Research confidential and general references
- Reference check performance with former supervisors and coworkers
- Verify credentials
- Consult on candidate resume
- Evaluate chosen final candidates

Candidate Preparation

- Review the job description
- Explain company culture and background
- Discuss unique challenges and expectations
- Give the background of the interviewing representatives

Client Interview Preparation

- Provide pre-interview and credential check information
- Discuss the interest points for the candidate
- Explain the candidate's concerns or reservations
- Relay the candidate's career goals
- Review client's interview process

Presenting the Candidates

- Arrange and coordinate interviewing schedules
- Showcase how the candidate fits the profile
- Explain the candidate's motivations
- Relay the candidate's interview availability

Candidate Debrief

- Get both positive and negative feedback from the candidate

▲

- Address specific questions left to be answered
- Assess interest in position
- Reiterate the pros of the position and client
- Gauge their interest in continuing this job order

Client Debrief

- Get feedback about the candidate post-interview
- Assess the qualification of the candidate
- Debrief on any potential incompatibilities or concerns
- Agree whether to pursue candidate or continue search
- Coordinate next step with hiring representative
- Arrange second interviews

Candidate Offer Consulting

- Prepare candidate for job offer
- Discuss required compensation package
- Gauge risk of counteroffer
- Discuss resignation date
- Agree upon desired start date
- Address any remaining concerns
- Review any details regarding possible relocations, etc.

Client Offer Consulting

- Strategize with client on negotiating an acceptable offer
- Consult desired compensation offer with client
- Review complete offer in detail (compensation package, bonus, etc)
- Review job specifics (relocation, title, responsibilities)
- Review desired start date
- Consult client on any concerns that would inhibit placement

Job Offer Presentation

- Facilitate and negotiate placement between candidate and client
- Confirm resignation date with candidate
- Confirm start date
- Review details for the placement in writing
- Assist candidate in professional resignation

Final Follow Up

- Remain in contact with both client and candidate until start date
- Confirm that candidate arrived on start date
- Follow-up with both client and candidate after start date
- Confirm with client that project is complete
- Ensure expectations are being met and both are satisfied
- Get agreement from client that they may be used as a future reference
- Maintain contact for periodic updates

A Day in the Life

Here, in a nutshell, is what a recruiter does. As we mentioned, the first order of business for any recruiter is to find work, which involves lots of phone calls to lots of companies. Once a recruiter lands a job order, she must then define the job with the client so she knows exactly what sort of candidate she should be looking for. Then she comes up with a list of names of possible candidates by calling people she knows in the industry to ask who might fit the bill—searching resume banks on the internet and approaching employees of competing companies with appropriate job titles.

Once she compiles a list of names, she calls everyone on the list to see if there's any interest in the position. She screens interested candidates with a telephone interview, looks over their resumes, and then selects the ones who are most appropriate. Then she'll conduct a formal interview, in person if possible. At this point, she may make background checks of criminal and financial records and verify college degrees. She may also speak with colleagues to make sure there are no skeletons in any closets. She refers all candidates who pass these tests to the client, sometimes giving them some tips on how to interview successfully. She also explains to the client why she believes the candidate is qualified. She waits while the company conducts interviews and chooses its candidate. If her candidate is chosen and accepts the position, the recruiter often helps negotiate salary, hiring bonuses, moving expenses, and so on.

In addition to the search process, the recruiter must keep up on her industry of specialty by reading the trade magazines and web sites and attending various trade functions.

Keep in mind that the recruiter is juggling several job orders at once. So while she's

> **Tip...**
>
> **Smart Tip**
> The Association of Executive Search Consultants (AESC) has a section dedicated to Industry Standards and their Code of Ethics is one of the highest regarded in the industry. Click to it: www.aesc.org.

Playing by the Rules

The National Association of Personnel Services has compiled a guide of ethical behavior for the recruiting industry. For a complete list, go to www.napsweb.org and look for Standards & Ethical Practices, under the About Us link. Here's a summary:

◯ Refer candidates to a client only when the client has given you permission to do so.

◯ Be as upfront with a candidate as possible about the hours, salary, and duties of a job.

◯ Take care in referring candidates to clients you know are engaging in questionable or illegal practices.

◯ Use information about candidates only for the purpose of finding them jobs.

◯ Let a candidate know if there is an impending strike or lockout before referring him or her to a company.

◯ Give clients an accurate description of a candidate's qualifications and skills. Let the client know if you cannot verify the accuracy.

◯ Keep confidential information about a client confidential.

◯ Do not try to recruit candidates from a client company unless the candidate has approached you.

compiling a list of possible candidates for one client, she's interviewing candidates for another client, and refining a job description with a third. All this while trying to drum up new business—and keep up with industry trends.

Like we said, it's a lot of time on the phone. And a lot of hours in the day. "Most good recruiters work from seven in the morning until seven in the night," Hawkinson says. "And most recruiters are on the phone seven days a week, because the best time to get a hold of candidates is at night or on weekends." See the Time Management Log on page 29 to help you organize your time.

Unfortunately, it's difficult not to work those kinds of hours. You need to be available to your clients and candidates 24/7. "It's hard to be a part-time consultant," Hawkinson says. "You never know what's going to happen. You have to be there. It's kind of like being a doctor in an emergency room. If a candidate decides he's going to turn a job down for some stupid reason, you can't let it go. You got to jump in immediately." If you can't convince him or her to accept, you'll lose the commission.

Tamara L. says she feels like she never leaves her work. "For me it's the hardest thing to leave here at 8 o'clock at night and drive to a happy hour at 8:30. But the wealth of connections is amazing."

Jeff H. who emphasizes the importance be self-disciplined and to organize your time wisely lays out his average day for us:

- Plans and makes his marketing business/client calls
- Makes his candidate recruiting calls
- Researches about companies online but doesn't use job boards
- Tracks his list of callbacks

Time Management Log

When you are getting into the swing of running your own desk, it's a good idea to map out your day. Below is a sample Time Management Log to keep your day organized.

Date: _____

Task	6 A.M.	7 A.M.	8 A.M.	9 A.M.	10 A.M.	11 A.M.	NOON	1 P.M.	2 P.M.	3 P.M.	4 P.M.	5 P.M.	6 P.M.

Find more forms for your business at www.entrepreneur.com/formnet.

- Creates To-Do List of 10–15 tasks to accomplish that day

He interviews candidates at night or on weekends so to not interfere with their workdays. The average interview takes 1.5 hours since long conversations during the day at a current job are suspicious. When he first started out, he worked at least 12 hour days and on Saturday and Sundays.

Stat Fact
Joseph Daniel McCool, editor of the Executive Recruiter News, estimates that most retained recruiters work 60 to 80 hours a week.

It's understandable; you have so much to juggle! You have to follow a process of steps so that you cover your bases to make a placement, make marketing calls for new job orders, source for candidates, interview candidates and prep them for interviews, debrief, and keep up with all those reference checks let alone check your email and get back to your voicemails.

Only you will know how to balance your workday, but here are some recommendations for lightening the load:

- *Create systems.* Right now, you may be scheduling all of your bills to be paid at the same time so you only need to worry about them once a month; do the same thing with your follow-up calls by creating a "tickler" file system to stay in touch with key contacts. The more you automate your workload, the less you'll have to think about it.

- *Prioritize.* There is the 80/20 rule for sales and then there's the 80/20 rule that says that 80 percent of whatever you deal with on a daily basis is a waste of your time. First things first, dedicate your time to the tasks that close deals and place urgent job orders before you get to another task that won't earn you a fee payment.

- *Defer.* If you can delegate or defer a task and have it done just as well or better, do it. You could spend hours and numerous emails trying to get an accurate job description or you can create a questionnaire to answer all of your questions.

If you are growing and you think you can support them, you might think of hiring some support staff. A healthy recruiter is a productive recruiter.

Smart Tip

Tip...

You may feel like you are tied to your desk, but a healthy body makes for a healthy mind. Try to get out and get 30 minutes of exercise at least three days a week. Even light exercise can combat stress and fatigue and keep burnout at bay.

Rewards and Pitfalls

The entrepreneurs interviewed for this book, social people that they are, not surprisingly said they like all the human contact involved in recruiting. "I meet some very, very nice people," says Donna K. "It's a very social line of work, which is wonderful."

"I love the connectivity of it," adds Tamara L. "The fact that you know someone everywhere. I like that everyone I'm working with can be my close personal friend."

They also like the matchmaking aspects of the job. "I help people find jobs they really want, and I help companies find people they really need—and look at this, oh wow! I get paid for it," says Donna. "That's really my approach to it. The day that I become all about money is the day I leave the business."

Smart Tip

Tip...

When you're on the phone all day, your voice can get awfully tired. To keep it in good shape, be sure to drink lots of water and avoid cigarette smoke. Also take care to speak at a natural level—shouting will wear out your voice box all too quickly.

"You get to make a major difference in the success of companies and the professional development and lives of individuals," agrees Ken C. The downside, says Ken, is the lack of control over whether a client accepts a candidate or a candidate accepts a job offer.

They also tire of the bad rap the profession gets. Many people view recruiters as vultures or thieves, eager to pull employees out of companies so they can make a buck. And the unethical and unprofessional recruiters cast a shadow over the whole profession. "Recruiting as a whole doesn't have a wonderful reputation," Donna says. "A lot of times I find it's an uphill battle to prove to people that I'm not sleazy, that I am reputable and ethical."

Plan Your
Launch

Once you get some background informa-
tion on whether getting into this industry is right for you, you

need to start planning how you want to launch your business.

In this industry, entrepreneurs typically choose to either buy a

franchise or start from scratch.

Buy the Training and the Business

Several companies sell recruiting franchises, which include intensive training and give you a name you can lean on. "I think the franchise deals are great," says Hawkinson of *The Fordyce Letter*, a newsletter for recruiters. "They put you through some pretty extensive training."

Mark M. says that even with training, "It takes at least 45 days to learn how to be a recruiter."

One of the entrepreneurs interviewed for this book, Larry D., in Huntersville, North Carolina, bought a franchise from Management Recruiters International (MRI). For $40,000 in 1993, Larry received training, assistance with opening his office, basic computer equipment, and a preliminary database.

Before he opened his office, Larry spent three weeks undergoing training, which included trying to find real clients and place a real candidate. He also learned about accounting and legal issues for recruiting firms. But he adds that he still had to build his client and candidate contacts. While the database he received with the purchase helped, "It really wasn't anything to scream about. Basically, you had to find your own jobs and your own candidates. It was pretty hard."

Larry decided to purchase the franchise because he didn't have any experience in recruiting and felt he needed the training and support. "I had never run a business before, and they had a pre-existing model that was successful," he says. "I liked the idea of learning a system and being around people who had done it and been successful. They have a built-in network of other MRI offices that you can share information and resources with." He continues to pay a 7.5 percent royalty on all commissions. In exchange, he receives support in running his business, including training employees and discounts on equipment and services. See the Basic Franchise Research Checklist below.

Basic Franchise Research Checklist

Franchise agreements vary among franchisors so it's hard to get a comprehensive list of aspects to investigate, but you want to do enough research to know what you are buying and your rights as a franchisee. Work with your lawyer to draft a franchise agreement or have them review the agreement provided by the franchisor. If you have reviewed the checklist and the agreement and it doesn't look like the right fit for you, you are not obligated to complete the transaction. Ask the following questions:

❑ What am I buying when I pay the franchise fee?

Basic Franchise Research Checklist, continued

- ❑ What is the payment schedule (lump payment or installments)?
- ❑ Does the franchisor offer any financing options?
- ❑ Is the initial fee refundable?
- ❑ Are there any royalty payment requirements? If so, what are they?
- ❑ What services does the franchisor provide in exchange for royalties?
- ❑ Does the franchisor offer co-op funds for advertising?
- ❑ Is there a starting capital requirement for operating expenses?
- ❑ Does the franchise agreement have a geographical requirement?
- ❑ Does the franchisee get to select the location or industry?
- ❑ Does the franchisor ensure no other franchisees compete in the same area or industry?
- ❑ What restrictions does the franchisor enforce?
- ❑ Does the franchisor cover insurance costs or offer insurance discounts?
- ❑ What training requirements does the franchisor require/offer?
- ❑ What control does the franchisor have over future operations?
- ❑ What cost advantages does the franchisor offer?
- ❑ Are there any hiring limitations?
- ❑ Does the franchisor have absolute control over the termination of the contract?
- ❑ If the contract is terminated, are there non-compete limitations?
- ❑ Can the franchisee sell the business and assign the franchise agreement to the buyer?
- ❑ Does the franchisor provide establishment assistance to comply with all federal and state legal requirements?

This is only a fraction of the questions your lawyer will want you to ask, but it's a good start to comparing a few franchise options. You essentially want to know the initial fee, capital required for operating costs, benefits provided by the franchisor, and the control that the franchisor will have over current and future operations.

Planning for Your Start-Up

Stat Fact

In 2006, there were 800 SCORE offices nationwide with over 10,000 counselors available to help.

Though buying a franchise may be a good way to enter the industry, most entrepreneurs start their own companies. This way, you can choose your specialty, industry, and do things your way from the start. So now you need to plan how you want to start your business.

Here is a checklist to hang onto while we explore how you start your own executive recruiting service. This is not everything you need to know, but it's always helpful to have a basic checklist to use along the way.

Entrepreneur's Start-Up Planning Checklist

Background Planning

- ❑ assess your strengths and weaknesses
- ❑ establish your personal and professional goals
- ❑ assess your financial resources
- ❑ identify the financial risks
- ❑ determine the start-up costs
- ❑ decide on your work location – home or office?
- ❑ do your target market research
- ❑ identify your clients
- ❑ identify your competitors
- ❑ develop a business plan
- ❑ develop a marketing plan

Business Transactions

- ❑ select a lawyer
- ❑ choose a business structure (sole proprietorship, partnership, corporation, etc.)

Entrepreneur's Start-Up Planning Checklist, continued

- ❏ create your business (register your business name, incorporate, etc.)
- ❏ select an accountant
- ❏ select a banker
- ❏ set up a business checking account
- ❏ apply for business loans (optional)
- ❏ establish a line of credit
- ❏ select an insurance agent
- ❏ obtain business insurance

First Steps of Implementation

- ❏ get business cards
- ❏ review local business codes
- ❏ get your furniture, equipment and software
- ❏ get a federal employer identification number (if you have employees)
- ❏ get a state employer identification number (if you have employees)
- ❏ send for federal and state tax forms
- ❏ join professional organizations and associations
- ❏ set a business opening date!

Mark McConnell, a successful executive recruiter who also started his own executive recruiting company and recently sold it says that if he were to mentor an entrepreneur planning a start-up in this industry he would recommend the following to focus on during the planning process:

- "Dumb down" your revenue projections and increase your expense forecast by at least 20 percent.
- Be prepared for adversity such as dealing with receivables, administrative tasks, and legal paperwork.
- Incorporate.
- There are excellent ways to do the business of recruiting; learn them if you don't already know them. Marketing your business, taking job orders, interviewing

candidates, prepping and debriefing, negotiations, etc.

- Specialize in something. No one goes to a general practitioner for heart surgery—specialists make more money.
- Don't cut corners in the placement process.
- Take the time to write a really compelling business plan.

Business Plan Basics

What is a business plan? A business plan explains your business goals, your strategies you'll use to meet them, the amount of money needed to start and keep going until you're profitable, and addresses any foreseeable problems.

Whether you are a seasoned professional and are just now opening your own doors or you're new to the industry, you need to start with a written business plan. This helps you think through what you're doing, see your strengths and weaknesses, and figure out a way to overcome challenges on paper before you actually have to face them in real life. Writing a business plan is a necessary chore; it's creating the foundation and setting the vision of your company. It won't make you an automatic success but it will bypass some common causes of business failure, such as unanticipated expenses or an inadequate marketing plan.

Mark M. says that his biggest mistake and regret was not writing a business plan. "Without a doubt, I should have written a more formal business plan which at the very least would have helped me remain more focused, and provided a daily operational roadmap for my actions and business decisions. Also, a formal business plan would have made it much easier to convey my value proposition to potential investors and seek additional funding. Take the time to write a really compelling business plan."

Tamara drew up a business plan before she went out on her own, even though she didn't plan to use it to obtain financing. She says, "I just wanted to be sure it was something that could work out." She showed it to colleagues in the business and adjusted it until it had everyone's approval.

There are three basic sections to a business plan: the business concept, the marketplace, and

Quick Quote

Unfortunately for Mark M., "I was advised by my mentors NOT to have a business plan, which in retrospect may have been one of my biggest mistakes."

the finances. If we look into these three sections further, you will find seven major components, not to mention a cover, title page, and table of contents:

1. Executive summary
2. Business description
3. Market strategies
4. Competitive analysis
5. Operations and management plan
6. Financial factors

Smart Tip Tip...

You can find sample business plans online that you can use as models for your own. Try a search using the keywords "business plan" and "writing," and you'll find a host of examples for plans.

Executive Summary

The executive summary should be written last because it basically sums up everything in the business plan as a condensed version of what's inside. Make sure you have completed everything else and then come back to the executive summary when you know what your main points are that you want to emphasize. When you do write it, it will tell the reader about the business, its business structure (sole proprietor, LLC, etc), the amount of money needed to launch, the repayment schedule if you are using a loan, what you would do with the loan and the equity balance after the loan, which is all much simpler if you are not looking for outside funding. The simpler the money situation, the easier the business plan will be. Remember that the executive summary should be only a page or less and make sure it sounds professional.

Business Description

Your business description is a great exercise for you since you are putting down all of your research that you've done in your planning stage. In this section, start with a description of the industry and its size. Explain why it's growing and what industry trends are causing that growth. Pull out statistics and industry information about why starting a business in this industry is a great opportunity.

Quick Quote

California entrepreneur Mark M. says "the issue of scalability is huge." You should plan for growth because the business is out there.

Market Strategies

Your market strategies section will be one of the factors that may best help you in this industry since there are so many competitors. In this section, describe your market—its size, structure, growth potential, trends, and sales (projects) potential. Use your research to focus on your future clients and the existing competition.

This may be a section to come back to once you narrow your specialty focus.

Competitive Analysis

Now check out the competition around you. Lay out the strengths and weaknesses of each one and pinpoint the strategies that will set you apart and emphasize how you can capitalize on those weaknesses. If you do your competitive

Smart Tip

Need more help? The Small Business Administration (SBA) has online tutorials and sample plans for you to check out. Go to www.sbaonline.sba.gov/ starting/indexbusplans.html.

analysis properly, you will prove that you have identified your competition and have come up with a plan to deal with them even if it's just being aware of them.

Operations and Management Plan

This section is for you to explain how you will run your business and who is involved. This section will be pretty short if you are the only one running the business, but even so, use this as a marketing section for you. Explain your role in the business and list your qualifications and what you will be managing.

Financial Factors

The financial statements are the backbone of your business plan and help keep the expense surprises to a minimum. This is your forecast in the short and long term and helps estimate how long until you are profitable.

You will need to draft an income statement, a cash flow statement, and balance sheet. The income statement details your cash-generating ability using revenue, expenses, depreciating capital, and cost of goods. Create a monthly income statement for your first year, then quarterly statements for the second year, and annual statements for the following years. Check out the Operating Income Worksheet on page 43.

Most businesses draft a five-year projection. The cash-flow statement tracks the money coming in and going out of your business in the same format as income statements (monthly, quarterly, then annually). This report will give you a profit or loss at the end of each term and then carry it over into the next report to show a cumulative amount. Watch this closely because if you see that you are cumulatively operating at a loss, it shows that you will need more capital than you first anticipated. Your balance sheet shows your venture's financial strength in terms of assets, liabilities, and equity. You only need to create one for each year, not monthly.

If there is any other important financial information not explained anywhere else in your business plan, such as your break-even point make sure to note it here. This section may seem the hardest to you but enlist the help of an accountant if you get stuck. It's important to give yourself a financial roadmap for your business, and it will help avoid money mishaps.

You may need to approach a bank if you decide to purchase a franchise, as these generally cost about $70,000. Larry D., the entrepreneur in Huntersville, North Carolina, purchased a franchise for $40,000 and elected to use his own cash. But if you do seek out a loan, it's best to have a business plan. A business plan is basically a description of the type of work you intend to do, where and how you intend to get clients, how you'll bill for your services, and how you plan to grow your business.

Beyond starting up and managing the day-to-day operations of your company, you need to think about the future. Even if all you want is to be a small, one-person shop, you need to have a plan to maintain your workload, income level, and client base.

The point is, no matter how busy you get in the present, you always need to have one eye on the future to assure the continuing success of your operation. Pull out your business plan every year and take another look at it. What has changed? What are your new goals? How has your business done in the past year compared to your projections? You should always be planning and working on improving your business and keeping an up-to-date business plan means that you know what it takes to make it profitable.

Understanding Financial Statements

One of the primary indicators of the overall health of your business is its financial status, and it's important that you monitor your financial progress closely. The only way you can do that is if you understand how to keep good records.

According to the Small Business Administration, you should prepare and understand some basic financial statements to track your growth and gauge the success of your business. You need to have a basic understanding of at least the following:

- *Cash flow budget.* This worksheet is used to project your cash in and cash out over the course of six months. By tracking your cash flow, you can predict shortages or abundance to possibly fund an expansion. It also tracks the changes on your balance sheet. This worksheet may be your most valuable financial management tool when running your own business.
- *Balance sheet.* This worksheet is your financial "snapshot" of your business at a certain period of time. This is a record of your assets, liabilities, and your business' net worth.
- *Profit and loss statement.* This example on page 42 shows your business over time and tracks the amount earned, how you spent it, and whether that caused a profit or a loss. You can purchase off-the-shelf accounting software that can help you create these reports.

Profit and Loss Statement

Placement Pals
January 20xx–December 20xx

Income

Sales	$85,950
Total Income	**$85,950**

Expenses

Bank service charges	$300
Dues and subscriptions	450
Insurance	1,000
Licenses and permits	75
Office supplies	1,025
Payroll	58,000
Professional fees	850
Rent	6,000
Telephone	1,200
Utilities	2,200
Total Expenses	**$71,100**
Net Income (Profit)	**$14,850**

- *Income statement.* The income statement summarizes all of your revenue sources compared to your business expenses for a given period of time.

You can handle the process manually or use any of the excellent computer accounting software programs on the market. You might want to ask your accountant for assistance getting your system of books set up. The key is to get set up and keep your records current and accurate throughout the life of your company.

Successful entrepreneurs review these reports regularly, at least monthly, so they always know where they stand and can move quickly to correct minor difficulties before they become major financial problems. If you wait until November to figure out whether or not you made a profit in February, you won't be in business for long.

Operating Income/Expense Planning Worksheet

Projected Monthly Income from Fees	$
Projected Monthly Expenses:	
Phone service	$
Cell phone plan	$
Internet service	$
Web site hosting (optional)	$
Marketing/advertising (minimal)	$
Transportation costs	$
Business insurance	$
Office supplies	$
Employee payroll and benefits	$
Loan repayment	$
Miscellaneous costs	$
If you are renting a commercial location:	
Rent	$
Utilities	$
Total Monthly Expenses	$
Projected Net Monthly Income	$

▲

But monitoring your financial progress takes discipline, particularly when you're growing fast and working hard. If you don't do it, warns an entrepreneur, you'll find yourself at the end of the year with nothing to show for your hard work and not knowing how to improve your profitability the following year.

Are You Restricted?

Savvy owners of recruiting firms have their employees sign noncompete clauses. These clauses prevent employees from competing with the employer for a period of time after the employees leave the firm. The restriction typically lasts from one to two years.

The noncompete usually applies only to the market your employer or former employer covers. So if you've signed a noncompete clause with an employer who specializes in placing chemical engineers in Texas, you may be able to place chemical engineers in California, or hospital administrators in Texas, just not chemical engineers in Texas.

What do you do if you've signed a noncompete and you want to go out on your own? "If you leave your employer," suggests Roger Linde, chairman of the National Association of Executive Recruiters, "start a recruiting firm in a new industry. [After all,] companies use your services because of your expertise in identifying people for them."

Another option—if you can afford it—is to take some time off to set up your business, and then start competing with your former employer once the noncompete period is over. Check with an attorney in your state before you sign a noncompete or leave an employer with whom you have a noncompete contract. Every state views noncompetes differently: "Some will enforce them to the letter," Linde says, "others will throw them out."

Entrepreneur Jeff H. was working for another recruiter when he wanted to leave due to a conflict of ethics. He didn't take any materials from his former company and instead spent time preparing his launch and his marketing. He had signed a noncompete clause to not do business within 100 miles of the company. To comply with his agreement, he signed a lease for an executive suite in another city 103 miles away and set up shop. He had developed stationery, identity, wrote a business plan, created business cards, and was up and running from day one.

Low Overhead

Now that you know how tough it is to get started in the recruiting industry, here's the upside. You'll need very little money to get going. "As long as you've got a telephone and a fax machine and a computer modem, you're in business," says Hawkinson. Add a printer for some business cards and official-looking stationery, and you're set.

Recruiting is an ideal homebased business. Almost all your work is done over the phone or on the internet. And when you want to interview candidates in person, you can do it in a restaurant or even at a social club. Entrepreneurs Manny A., Ken C., and Vivian K. (who runs a recruiting firm in Philadelphia) all work out of their homes. And Tamara L. started her business in her home.

Your start-up costs could be fairly minimal if you already have a computer and a fax machine at home. Don't forget, however, that your phone bills will be very high— $600 a month or more—as you'll be making many calls to clients, especially in the beginning.

5

Taking Aim at
Your Market

If you feel like you have what it takes to start a
recruiting business—search experience, an outgoing personality and an ability to sell—the next step is to do a little market
research. Because the field is growing so rapidly, it's a safe bet
that the work is out there. To find it, you'll need a little—no,
make that a lot of—persistence. But you'll be ahead of the

game if you can determine beforehand what your specialty will be and which companies you'll target as your clients. In this chapter, we'll give you some tools to help you figure out where your market lies.

Room for One More

All the recruiters interviewed for this book said they didn't worry about being able to find work. Tamara L. in San Mateo, California, who does both contingency and retained recruiting, said that when she left the recruiting firm she was working for, "We were turning down clients left and right. We couldn't get to them. I felt supremely confident that we'd be able to turn it around in three months at the latest. I genuinely had no concern about getting a client base."

Donna K. in New York, who left a small search firm to start her own contingency-only firm, adds that she knew she could drum up plenty of business "because I had a lot of clients. As soon as I put the word out there that I had created a new company, I had quite a few solicitations to work on jobs."

Larry D., who does contingency and retained recruiting in Huntersville, North Carolina, had no experience in recruiting before he opened his business. But even he wasn't concerned about finding clients. He just hit the phones, calling as many as 80 companies a day, until he started finding work. "There are a billion recruiters out there, but there are very few good ones," he advises. That means companies are always looking for a recruiter who can deliver quality candidates.

"The work is always there," agrees Hawkinson of *The Fordyce Letter*. "If you make enough phone calls, you'll find a company willing to hire you."

While the consensus is that if you apply yourself, you'll find plenty of work, it does help if you focus your search somewhat.

Specialty of the Business

Nearly everyone in the recruiting business has a specialty, a field within which they place candidates. The field may be a type of industry, such as the clothing trade or wastewater engineering, or it may be a type of job that cuts across different industries—information technology professionals or marketing managers, for example.

How do you pick a niche or specialty? Mark M. shares, "You either focus on an industry—like semiconductors or entertainment, or you focus on a function like accounting, HR, IT, or legal. Choose something you are passionate about and that makes sense based on your personal bio. For example, I was an accountant prior to becoming a recruiter. If you focus on an industry, you will most likely need to cast a

Smart Tip

Tip...

A good specialty may be one in which you have lots of contacts, even if you've never worked in that business. Say many of your friends are attorneys; they can always refer you to potential clients and candidates in their field. For you, then, placing lawyers may work out well.

national net for clients and candidates and will do 90 percent of your placements over the phone. If you focus functionally, you can work with any company in any industry and would work a local market."

"What we've found is that the expertise is not necessarily only in the industry. It's in the specifics of the job," says Vivian K., who does retained searches in Philadelphia. For example, her firm places many human resources personnel—these are people whose skills work as well for manufacturing as they do for publishing or medicine. But Vivian notes that, "It does help to have a specialty in booking business. When a client is talking to you, they want to know that you specialize in their industry." Having a specialty in one area shows your clients that you're well connected in that field, so you can make a good placement quickly.

"If you're a specialist in left-handed widgets, and all the left-handed widget professionals know that you specialize in that area," says Hawkinson, "then you build up an inventory of professionals who want to use your services because they know you're tapped into the left-handed widget companies. And the left-handed widget companies want to use you because they know you're tapped into the left-handed widget professionals."

A Clean Break

Recruiters who leave old firms to start new ones, even if they never signed a noncompete clause, still need to be careful about how they find new clients. Taking databases, Rolodexes, files, business cards, or anything else with information about clients could constitute stealing. See the Sample Noncompete Agreements on pages 166 and 167.

Donna K. from New York didn't have a noncompete to worry about, but she was careful not to take any business property from her former employer. She left all her clients' contact information with her former employer, and then took out a newspaper ad letting clients know she was starting a new business. Once they contacted her, she added them to the database of her new business. If she had taken a database of client phone numbers and addresses and mailed out announcements, she said, her former employer "could have had legal recourse."

But besides helping you sell yourself to clients, specializing can save you precious time. "It's best to have a specialty," says Hawkinson. "That way, you don't have to keep re-creating the wheel every time you get a new job order."

You'll likely find that you'll be trying to fill different positions with the same job description, so if you have some candidates who weren't hired for one position, you can refer them for another one without having to go through the search and screening process again. "A lot of jobs I work on have the same exact description," says Donna K., "so I could conceivably be sending the same candidate to five different jobs." Because she's working on a contingency basis, she's under no obligation to refer a candidate to only one client. Donna adds that if more than one client wants to hire a candidate, she lets the candidate choose which job will work out the best.

So how do you choose a specialty? Many recruiters specialize in fields they worked in formerly. Donna left the market research field to recruit in market research. "I don't think I would have become a recruiter if it was recruiting for an industry I was unfamiliar with," she says. Because she had worked in market research, she had many contacts in the field, which made it easier for her to find clients and candidates. Also, because she understood the industry, she knew how to interview candidates and measure their knowledge and skill in the field.

Tamara L. also leveraged the knowledge she gained from her previous field, management consulting, when she started recruiting. "Having knowledge of that space

---

How Do You Switch a Specialty?

You don't have to change over completely but you might want to start transitioning if you see your current specialty drying up. Here are some tips when picking a new specialty:

- ❍ *Look for long-term necessity.* Find a niche or specialty that could become obsolete in five years.
- ❍ *Check your interest level.* If you aren't even remotely interested in the industry, culture or candidates, then you won't want to spend 80 hours a week advancing their careers.
- ❍ *Give yourself time.* It will take time to gain the trust of clients to close on job orders so be patient when you're building relationships and rapport.
- ❍ *Recognize the ramp up.* It will also take time to get up to speed. Remember that your goal is to arrange sendouts to get candidates in front of your clients. The more interviews you have with candidates, the more people you have available to send out.

really worked for me," she says. "I really homed in on that skill set. I did branch out and start working other areas, but I always kept that as my core area."

Other recruiters find that they fall into a specialty. Hawkinson tells a story about a colleague who decided to specialize in chemical process engineering. This recruiter started calling human resources departments at chemical process companies saying he was a recruiter specializing in this area. He didn't get any contracts to fill, but one human resources worker he contacted said he was looking for a job, so the recruiter found him a position. "The next thing you know, he's an HR specialist," Hawkinson says.

Some recruiters also find that their specialties evolve. They may work in one area for a while and then gravitate toward an industry they're more interested in. They may move into other fields when a loyal client switches industries and asks the recruiter to fill positions in that field. Or they'll move into a more lucrative area when another starts to dry up.

So your specialty can be a field about which you're already knowledgeable, one in which you have many contacts, or even one that you're interested in and about which you're willing to learn. It helps to have previous contacts and industry knowledge, but you can learn about a field by reading trade publications and meet people by joining industry associations and simply talking with professionals. See the Specialty Worksheet on page 57 to get you started thinking about the right specialty for your executive recruiting business.

For recruiting, choosing a specialty is part of developing a marketing plan, something all entrepreneurs should do before hanging out a shingle.

Making a Specialty Selection

You may already have a specialty or a few ideas for specialties. Now it's time to think about which one will work out. You'll need to

▲

know whether your prospective specialty is growing or shrinking. Also, you'll want to find out if hiring managers in your field use recruiters. And you should consider the possibility that there may be too many recruiters in that specialty already.

Be sure to pick a specialty that's growing—or at least stable. In a growing field, the recruiters who have already staked a claim will have their hands full, and you can pick up the slack. If, after a few years, the specialty hits a slump, you'll at least be established with loyal clients and a network of contacts.

On the other hand, if you choose a specialty that's shrinking, you'll be competing with recruiters who have worked in the field for years and are desperately holding onto those few jobs that come their way. It will be much more difficult to find work.

More and more businesses, and more and more types of businesses, are using recruiters, so don't rule out any specialty because it hasn't traditionally used recruiters. Some industries just haven't awakened to the fact that recruiters can save them money and time. Your sales skills may be able to convince them to give you a try.

Whether the industry traditionally uses recruiters or not, and whether it's even growing or shrinking, the rule of thumb is that a good specialty is one in which employees are difficult to find. Companies often turn to recruiters when they can't

Drawing Boundaries

Thanks to e-mail, faxes, and cell phones, you can work just about anywhere and place candidates in companies just about anywhere else. Larry D., in Huntersville, North Carolina, says most of his clients are in Chicago and New York City. Ken C., who works in Panama City Beach, Florida, takes on clients from anywhere in the nation.

But other entrepreneurs interviewed for this book found that limiting their geographic scope has helped them focus their business. Donna K. in New York City, for example, stays within the general New York City area. Doing so focuses her potential client list and keeps her well connected in the New York market research world. And unlike Ken, who travels around the country to interview candidates, Donna can interview all her candidates in person in her own office.

If you're in a large metropolitan area, you may be able to confine your market within that area if you think that will benefit you. This is especially true if your industry is concentrated in one area—if, for example, you're recruiting for the entertainment industry in Los Angeles or for the publishing industry in New York. But if you're in the boondocks, you'll probably have to go regional or even national.

Bright Idea

You may think you want to go after the positions with big salaries, since you'll receive a percentage. But lower-level jobs are often much easier to fill, so they're an ideal way to start recruiting. And as your placements move up the ladder, so will you.

find workers on their own. So if, in your chosen field, hopeful employees are lining up, resumes in hand, just to get their foot in the door, you'd probably be better off finding another field. It needn't be radically different: Perhaps the companies you've targeted have no problem filling entry-level positions, but are desperate for people who have managed a crew or had a few years mastering the equipment.

The best way to find out if your field is going to yield you a mile-long client list is to run a market survey, targeting some hiring managers within the field. Get the names of the men and women who are hiring in your field. You can also talk to human resources departments.

Call them and ask how many positions they have open, whether they use recruiters, what rate they pay if they do, and what positions they have a difficult time filling. Try to get an understanding of how high the turnover is. Also ask if they like to hire on retainer or on contingency. Keep it brief—you don't want to annoy them or make them feel you're wasting their time. These are the people who will be giving you business.

If you're finding that many companies have few positions open and expect very little turnover, then that specialty may not yield enough work for you. If your interviewees say they never use recruiters, ask them why. If it just hasn't been their practice, perhaps they'd be willing to give your services a try, especially if you're working on a contingency basis. But if they say they don't use recruiters because they have no trouble filling positions, it's likely that the market for that specialty isn't in your favor.

Be sure to ask them if there are any positions in the company that are difficult to fill. There's a good chance that if one company is having trouble filling a certain position, others are as well. Say your chosen specialty—accountants for widget manufacturers—wasn't such a good idea after all. Widget accountants are a dime a dozen. But, as it turns out, widget manufacturers are having a terrible time finding designers to create the next line of widgets. That means widget designers could become your specialty area for recruiting.

Smart Tip

Tip...

Whenever a potential client takes the time to fill you in on the industry buzz, be sure to send a short thank-you note afterward. They'll appreciate your kindness and remember you as ethical and courteous—an important step toward getting business.

Ask about payment methods: A company that hires only retained searchers is probably going to be harder to break into than a company that hires on a contingency basis. When they use contingency, it doesn't cost them anything to try out a new recruiter.

It's important, also, to ask what the company pays its recruiters. If clients refuse to pay more than 20 percent of a placement's salary, you know there are already too many recruiters working in that field. Find another specialty; you can't make it on 20 percent commission. See the Client Survey Worksheet on page 56 to help you develop and organize your telephone market survey.

The Best Specialty Bets

Once you know your specialty—say it is recruiting health-care administrators—where do you find the clients? Naturally, you'll target the companies that hire health-care administrators: hospitals, insurance companies, health maintenance organizations and physician groups. But you can refine your target client list a little better by thinking about who is likely to need your services.

The ideal client is a big company with lots of assets that will barely blink when it writes out your five- or six-figure check. "Big businesses. Real big businesses," says

---

The Client Locator

It may seem too simple, but the best place to start looking for potential clients is your local library. If you've chosen vintners as your specialty, for example, you'll want to get a list of wineries. Tell the librarian that you're looking for a list of wineries within a certain area or even nationally, if that's your target.

He or she can help you find your industry's SIC (Standard Industrial Classification) code, then show you how to find companies fitting that code in a number of directories—S&P 500 Index, Directory of Corporate Affiliations, Thomas Register or others. The library may also have directories published by industry associations.

In addition to helping you compile a list of companies, a librarian can help you find more indepth information about individual companies, such as annual reports and media coverage. These will help you determine whether the client is worth pursuing.

McCool of Executive Recruiter News, "with millions and billions of dollars to spend on recruitment." Not only do these companies have lots of cash to give you, but they're also accustomed to hiring recruiters. But McCool warns that the competition for the really big companies is intense.

"Everybody's after the same clients, frankly," he says. He adds that some smaller companies, especially growth companies, may be more accessible to new recruiters. These companies won't have so many recruiters calling them, and they may not already have a pool of recruiters working for them. Another good target is companies that are growing, since they're filling positions. And, of course, you want companies that often have trouble filling key positions.

A company that is laying off employees may sound like a bad idea, but don't be too hasty to write it off. It may be phasing out one area of its business, say textbook development, but developing another area—video production, for example. If you're placing video editors or producers, you're in business.

Read up on your area of specialty: Peruse the business pages of local and national papers, subscribe to trade magazines, and search for companies online. If you keep up on the news, you'll know which companies will make the best targets.

Client Survey

By doing a little market research before you hang out a shingle, you'll greatly increase your chances of success. This quick phone market survey will guide you to the best specialty and best clients. Call human resources personnel or the managers who hire people in the positions you're hoping to fill. Be extremely courteous; always ask if it's a good time to talk. If not, ask if you can set up a date at a later time.

1. How many positions do you have open at this time?_____

2. What are those positions? _____

   _____

3. How many employees in those positions have been with you less than a year?

   _____

4. How many positions do you expect to have open a year from now? _____

   _____

5. How often do you hire from outside sources?_____

6. What positions do you have the most difficulty filling? _____

   _____

7. Do you employ the services of recruiters? _____

   If you do not, why not? _____

   _____

   If you do:

   ○ Would you be willing to try out a new recruiter? _____

   ○ Do you hire on a contingency or retainer basis? _____

   ○ What percentage do you pay? _____

Specialty Worksheet

Use this worksheet to help you choose the right specialty for your executive recruiting firm.

List three specialties with which you are familiar:

1. _____
2. _____
3. _____

List three industries that are concentrated in your geographic area:

1. _____
2. _____
3. _____

List three industries or specialties that are growing:

1. _____
2. _____
3. _____

Choosing one specialty at a time, start going down the checklist below. If you repeated any specialties in the lists above, those are probably the most promising and the best to start with.

❑ Make a list of all the contacts you have in that specialty. The more, the better.
❑ Check with any recruiters you know and see if they have any sense about whether your ideas for specialties will work.
❑ Read trade journals to see how the industry or specialty is doing.
❑ Check with your library to see how many companies would hire people in your specialty.
❑ Call as many potential clients as you can and ask them questions listed in the "Client Survey" included in this chapter on page 56.

If all your research about a particular specialty gives you a green light, give it a try. You can always try another one if it doesn't work out.

Setting Up
Shop

Once you've researched your market and chosen a specialty, it's time to look at where you want to run your recruiting business. In this chapter, we'll discuss the advantages of working at home vs. out of an office space. It's important to choose an option that works best for you and your budget.

▲

Where the Magic Happens

Your work space can be as simple as a corner of your bedroom, or as elaborate as an office suite. It all depends on your tastes and how much you want to grow and spend.

In the executive recruiting business, there's no reason to move to an office space initially.

Being homebased has the considerable advantages of low cost and great convenience. You avoid paying rent on commercial office space and you get to deduct a percentage of your mortgage or rent from your taxes. Besides, you don't have to commute, you can play fetch with your dog while you're on hold, and sort laundry while waiting for a return call. However, keep in mind that if you're interviewing candidates, pitching your services or otherwise working connections, you need to take copious notes and stay on the ball, so your full attention is well advised.

Vivian K. runs a recruiting firm of seven people in the Philadelphia area, and all of them work from their homes. They get together twice a week for strategy meetings, but the rest of the time they communicate through phone and e-mail. She says one of the main advantages for her is that she doesn't commute, which is especially important because she has two young children. "When I'm finished with work, I can be with my kids five minutes later," she says.

Vivian adds that she can easily respond to any problem or issue that arises. "I can do whatever I need to do whenever," she says. "I'll just wake up in the middle of the night, and I'll have an idea, and I'll be downstairs working for a few hours." Meeting with clients and candidates hasn't been a problem for her, either. She notes that, "If you're really learning about your client, you want to see them on their turf." And when she interviews candidates, she meets them in a restaurant or cafe, or even a club in an airport terminal.

Ken C., our Florida recruiter who works at home, also rents space in airports and hotels when he interviews candidates. He usually travels to meet them anyway, so he's not going out of his way finding a private space to talk.

Choosing Your Business Location

When it comes to the actual site of your business, you have two choices: homebased or a commercial location. An executive recruiting service company can be extremely successful in

> **Stat Fact**
> According to the Small Business Administration, experts estimate that at least 20 percent of new small businesses are homebased.

Smart Tip Tip...

If you're working out of your home, try to set up a separate room for your business. It'll make it easier to concentrate on work if you're not looking at all the housework you could be doing. Also, to deduct a home office for tax reasons, your work space must be dedicated exclusively to your business.

either venue; your decision will depend on your individual resources and goals.

In any business, but especially in this one, a professional image is a critical element of success. Homebased operations are very accepted in today's business world but you still need to present the appearance of being a serious business, even though you may choose to work from your house. And if you opt for a commercial location, be sure it is one that is compatible with your goals.

Many operators start from home with the goal of moving into commercial space as soon as they're established with a few clients, and this is an excellent strategy if you are planning to expand and hire employees.

Homebased Operations

The major benefit of starting a homebased business is the fact that it significantly reduces the amount of start-up and initial operating capital you'll need. But there's more to consider than simply the upfront cash. You need to be conveniently located so you can minimize travel time.

Next, think about your home itself. Do you have a separate room for an office, or will you have to work at the dining room table? Can you set up a comfortable workstation with all the tools and equipment you'll need? Can you separate your work area from the rest of the house so you can have privacy when you're working and get away from "the office" when you're not?

Entrepreneur.com provides numerous resources for homebased businesses and it has developed a Home Office Worksheet on page 62 to help you locate and design your home office space:

Commercial Appeal

While working at home is a perfectly viable option, there are some instances when you may want to rent a dedicated office space. If you have a small apartment or house, renting office space will make you feel less cramped at home. You may find that you focus better if you separate your home and work life. At an office, the bored dog, unsorted laundry, and wilting gardenias won't steal attention away from your work.

Home Office Worksheet

List three possible locations in your home for your office, which should include a work area for you and enough space for your desk, computer, and telephone:

1. _____

2. _____

3. _____

Make a physical survey of each location:

○ Are phone and electrical outlets placed so that your equipment can easily access them? Or will you be faced with unsightly, unsafe cords snaking across the carpet?

_____

_____

○ Measure your space. Will your current desk or table (or the one you have your eye on) fit? _____

_____

○ Do you have adequate lighting? If not, can you create or import it? Is there proper ventilation? _____

_____

○ What is the noise factor? _____

_____

○ Is there room to spread out your work? _____

_____

○ Optional: How close is it to the coffeemaker? Refrigerator? (This can be either a plus or minus, depending on your current jitter factor and waistline.) _____

_____

Home Office Worksheet, continued

Next, list three possible home locations for your supplies and files:

1. _____

2. _____

3. _____

Again, make a survey of each location:

○ Is it climate-controlled? Will you need climate control? _____

_____

○ Is there adequate lighting, ventilation, and space for you to easily access your inventory? _____

_____

○ Will you need to construct special shelving or add other storage space? If so, make notes here: _____

_____

_____

_____

There's a flip side to working at home, admits Vivian. "What's bad about it is I can do whatever I need to do whenever." she says. "I have a tendency to work a lot. It doesn't separate your life as much."

Having an office space outside your home may help if you'll be interviewing lots of candidates locally, as they can just come by your office. Donna K., the New York City recruiter, has all her candidates come by her office for interviews, saving her a good deal of time—especially if someone's a no-show.

If you do want to interview candidates in your office, look for a location that's accessible—with parking or near public transportation—and in a relatively nice neighborhood. Tamara L., who rents office space with her partners in San Mateo,

California, chose that city because it was near her and her partners' homes. It's also centrally located for her clients, most of whom are in the San Francisco Bay Area. "I wanted to be available to the whole Bay Area," she says.

The office location really doesn't matter if you're not planning on seeing candidates in your office. Whatever is convenient for you and your employees is just fine. The recruiters interviewed for this book said that clients didn't seem to care where their offices were located. Besides, as Manny A., our recruiter in Chicago points out, "The client really doesn't know if you're working out of your house or you're working out of an office."

Regardless of the specific place, a commercial location gives you a degree of credibility that is hard to earn in a homebased office. You'll also have more space and will be able to create a setup that is more efficient and practical than what you might be able to do in a spare bedroom. You'll probably only need 200 to 400 square feet at first, and you should be able to find an office that size in a good location at a fairly reasonable price. Sharing office space with a noncompeting or complementary business to save money may also be an option.

So, whether you rent or work out of your home is really a matter of personal choice. Some of the entrepreneurs interviewed for this book work out of their homes; others rent office space. And others mix it up: Manny maintains office space where his assistant works, but he spends most of his time working from home. The office rental

Office Options

If getting out of the house is your main goal in renting office space, there's no reason to go for fancy digs. Whatever's cheap and convenient can work for you, as you can always meet with clients at their location and interview candidates at a restaurant.

Maybe a friend has a garage he or she never uses and is willing to let you use it for a nominal fee, or even in trade. You may even find someone willing to rent out an extra bedroom that you can use while the owner is at work during the week. Also, many businesses rent more space than they need and sublet extra cubicles to entrepreneurs like you.

Check local newspapers and community bulletin boards, and ask around. All you need is about 100 square feet of space. Remember, you'll be on the phone quite a bit, so be sure your chatting won't bother your officemates.

market varies wildly depending on your location, but you can count on paying between \$1 and \$5 a square foot, each month.

There's no reason you can't change your mind after you try one tack. You can always have the phone line forwarded, or, if you have a cell phone, the number won't change.

Office Swank and Décor

A number of factors will influence how you arrange your office. Your layout depends on whether you are homebased or in a commercial location, and if you are a one-person shop, or have employees and so forth. Given all the variables involved, it's impossible to suggest an ideal, one-size-fits-all layout. But there are some points you need to consider. An example of this is if you are interviewing candidates in your commercial office, you will need an enclosed, semi-soundproofed area that allows privacy and confidentiality.

Your office décor should be businesslike, efficient, and attractive. You don't need to spend a lot of money on elegant furnishings, but you do need to make sure you create a favorable impression in your clients' and candidates' minds. A good coat of paint will go a long way in brightening up your environment. Neutral shades such as beige or muted gray are good choices and will let you highlight your interior with bold graphics, posters, art prints, or bulletin boards. A few large plants will also add to the ambience, but be sure you maintain them.

Desks and chairs should be attractive and functional but not excessively luxurious. Invest in ergonomically sound chairs and equipment to preserve your health and productivity—and that of your employees. Be sure trash cans are emptied regularly and that the office is kept clean and dusted. Periodically take a look at your office through the eyes of a client who has never seen it before, and think about the impression it makes.

Tools of the
Trade

This is where recruiters have it easy. There are so few tools needed to become a recruiter, you're likely to have everything in your home already. Chances are, you find a trip to your local office supply superstore more exciting than a day at the mall, but resist the temptation to get carried away with exotic gadgets and "office toys." Think carefully about what you need—and don't need—do your homework, and make your buying decisions wisely.

Equip Yourself for Success

Essentially, the job calls for a phone. Consider a headset for comfort and efficiency. Your telephone itself can be a tremendous productivity tool, and most of the models on the market today are rich in features that you will find useful. Such features include automatic redial, which redials the last number you called at regular intervals until the call is completed; programmable memory for storing frequently called numbers; and a speakerphone for hands-free use. You may also want call forwarding, which allows you to forward calls to another phone number when you are not at your desk, and call waiting, which signals you that another call is coming in while you are on the phone. These services are typically available through your telephone company for a monthly fee.

The phone service will run you about $25 a month with a line installation fee of $40 to $60. A good phone, with auto-redial, memory dial, and two lines, is what you'll

Can You Hear Me Now?

Your cell phone is your lifeline to your business whenever you are away from your desk. Because the phone number doesn't change, you can change offices without losing any clients or connections. You can have your cell phone pick up if your business phone isn't answered, and vice versa, so you don't have to give everyone three or four different phone numbers. You will want to pick a rate plan that supports your call volume and a service provider that has strong cell service in your area. Not much is worse than dropping a call with a client when they thought you were at your office. Some of the top-of-the-line phones now offer online services such as e-mail and internet access. Don't go for a fancy phone if you aren't going to use all of the extra added features. A cell phone costs about $100 with a charge of about $50 a month, depending on how many minutes you want to use it.

You don't need to purchase
stationery unless you want to
use logos or other images on
letterhead and envelopes.
Word-processing programs
and printers let you produce
professional-looking letters
and envelopes. Some pro-
grams even include artwork.

want. (You'll be living on the phone.) That'll
cost you between $70 and $150. It's better to
get an answering service rather than an
answering machine: You don't want to miss
calls—or even interrupt calls when your call
waiting beeps. An answering service costs
between $6 and $20 a month. So, for less than
$200 on phone equipment and $50 a month on
charges, you could be in business.

A computer is an obvious necessity that you
will need to conduct research, use databases,
write letters, and send and receive e-mail. The
basic requirements for a computer should be
either a PC with a Pentium 4 or Celeron 2.8 or higher processor running Windows
XP. If prefer using a Mac, which isn't recommended because most of your clients will
be using a PC, you need an Apple G3 or higher with Mac OS X.

Last but not least, make sure your internet connection is 56K or faster. You'll be
spending a lot of time corresponding by email and researching online, so invest in
high-speed internet. The packages these days may be able to bundle your phone line
with your internet service to save you money. Be sure to shop around.

Your Office Needs

There are, of course, several additional
items that will make your job much easier. Use
the Office Supplies Checklist on page 71 to
help you keep track. A fax machine will let you
receive and send resumes stat. It'll cost you
between $100 and $250, unless you want to get
a combination fax/ copier/printer/scanner,
which costs between $250 and $800.

A paper shredder is now a must-have item. A
response to both a growing concern for privacy
and the need to recycle and conserve space in
landfills, shredders are becoming increasingly
common in both homes and offices. They allow
you to efficiently destroy incoming unsolicited
direct mail, as well as sensitive documents

Got the Goods?

On the subject of equipment, there are a couple of issues you need to think about carefully before making the final decision on what to buy—and how to pay for it.

❍ *Used or new.* Most of the operators we talked with preferred to buy new when it comes to computers, printers, and other equipment used in the delivery of their services. Though used equipment is usually a bargain from a price perspective, the technology is often out of date. The price may be much cheaper, but the reliability of used equipment is not worth the money saved. Furnishings such as desks, chairs, filing cabinets, and various office fixtures are a different story. These items can safely be purchased used at a substantial savings through dealers, classified ads, and other sources.

❍ *Lease or buy.* With computers and peripherals becoming increasingly affordable, the leasing option is becoming decreasingly viable. Most leasing companies don't want to bother with a single computer-and-printer package, and business owners find it makes more financial management sense to buy the equipment.

before they are discarded. Make sure that you get a 'cross cut' shredder since the less expensive types only cut the paper lengthways.

A printer, which costs from $250 to $500 for an inkjet and from $500 to $2,000 for a laser, will let you send official-looking reports and contracts. You probably don't need the higher-end printers—these are for designers and publishers who need exceptionally high-quality color reprints of photographs and images. All you need is a printer that will produce good quality black-and-white paper documents.

A desk ($200 to $600) and a chair ($60 to $250) will keep you comfortable, and a filing cabinet ($25 to $100) will keep your papers in order. Pens, paper, sticky notes, correction fluid, and the usual little office supplies will set you back about $200. Business cards and business stationery will run about $200 to $400.

As for software, you'll want a word processing system ($85 to $250) most of all. Be sure to get a popular system such as Microsoft Word so you can share files easily. When someone e-mails a resume, you want it to look like a resume, not a sheet of hieroglyphics. It's helpful for bookkeeping purposes to have an accounting program such as Quicken. This will set you back between $80 and $250.

Office Supplies Checklist

Use this checklist to make sure you have what you need to start your recruiting business.

Basics

❑ Telephone $_____

❑ Cell phone   _____

❑ Answering service   _____

❑ Computer   _____

❑ Fax machine   _____

❑ Printer   _____

❑ Desk   _____

❑ Chair   _____

❑ Filing cabinet   _____

❑ Internet access   _____

❑ Database software   _____

❑ Word processing software   _____

❑ Headset   _____

❑ Stationery/business cards   _____

❑ Accounting software   _____

Extras

❑ Shredder   _____

❑ Scratch pads   _____

❑ Staplers, staples, and staple remover   _____

❑ Tape and dispenser   _____

❑ Scissors   _____

❑ "Sticky" notes in an assortment of sizes   _____

❑ Paper clips   _____

❑ Plain paper for your copier and printer   _____

❑ Paper and other supplies for your fax machine   _____

❑ Pens, pencils, and holders   _____

❑ Trash cans   _____

❑ Desktop document trays   _____

❑ Labels   _____

Total Office Supplies Expenditures: $_____

In addition to purchasing software, you'll also need programs that will handle your accounting, client information management, and other administrative requirements. Software can be a significant investment, so do a careful analysis of your own needs and then study the market and examine a variety of products before making a final decision. Here are three other items to consider adding to your business set-up:

- *Business card scanner*. If you are going to be collecting a bunch of business cards (if you're networking like you should be, you will!), a scanner can be a tremendous productivity tool because it can save you hours of information entry.

- *Data-backup systems*. To protect your database, you need to routinely perform a backup. Your computer vendor can help you choose a backup system compatible with your computer.

- *Uninterruptible power supply*. To protect your computer system as well as any work you have open, all of your machines should be plugged into an uninterruptible power supply that will provide electricity in the event of a power failure. These devices also provide a degree of protection against power surges.

Creating an Online Presence

Setting up a web site for your recruiting business could definitely be worth your while. It could help your clients or candidates learn more about your business. And it may help you appear legitimate and professional—always helpful when you're starting out.

But the recruiters we interviewed say don't count on it drawing any business your way. Several have web sites that they'll mention to their clients, but they stress that they still have to find clients the old-fashioned—and difficult—way: cold calls and networking. Manny A. in Chicago says, "I have a web site, but it doesn't bring in a lot of business."

Vivian K. in Philadelphia concedes: "It doesn't get business. It's a way of being on the map, like any brochure-ware."

Mark M. in California says "Do your web site well. It is the face of your business that shows your professionalism and may give the impression that it's a larger company. It doesn't have to be expensive but it needs to be done well."

If you have a web site, you can place the address on your business cards and any other stationery, and let potential clients refer to it. Be sure to state your specialty and any regional focus on your site, and mention how many years you have in the business if it's an impressive number. Don't list your clients on your web site unless they give you the green light to do so.

One last tip would be to offer some free tools on your site that bring more traffic such as tips or recommendations or use it to help your candidates beautify their resumes. Put some templates on your site of professional resumes you've seen, and it will save you some editing time.

Technology in the Recruiting Industry

Most of the entrepreneurs interviewed for this book swear by their databases. They use a variety of products, some of them designed specifically for executive recruiters, which manage all their contacts. These programs run as low as $500 and as much as tens of thousands of dollars. Paul Hawkinson of *The Fordyce Letter* says $500 database software will serve you as well as the more expensive names. These products, including ACT, Paradox, Goldmine, and Access, can be purchased at any computer store.

Donna K., the recruiter in New York City, says that with her program, "You can put in every piece of information possible. You code candidates in terms of their skills, their salaries, their titles, where they work. It essentially manages your day."

Mark M. has created this breakdown for the technology for the recruiting industry and how it has changed:

The advent of the Job boards such as Monster, Careerbuilder, and a million other niche sites are still only electronic newspapers and will never replace recruiters. They show you the 3 percent of the workforce that is unemployed or often unemployable! They represent a "passive" approach for companies in their recruiting efforts. Companies that use these sites are often flooded with unqualified emails and resume responses and still have to sift through these anyway. Recruiters seek out the "other 97 percent" of workers out there who are employed and NOT seeking a new position. Giving clients access to these potential candidates is the essence of what headhunters bring to the party.

There are some great software packages out there as well as web-based solutions. Even an off-the-shelf package such as ACT! Or Goldmine can be customized for use in a recruiting firm and can be expanded to multi-user use as well. Web based solutions such as Salesforce.com or Bullhorn are worth looking into as well and usually charge a monthly fee. Two other software programs to check out are RecruitMax or MicroJ. Many of these recruiting technologies make many activities such as searching for specific candidates, emailing resumes, and tracking follow up calls a snap.

Internet Research is a science—using the internet to mine for candidate names, potential sales leads, industry updates, and bulletins and information on client companies is critical. Many recruiting firms have researchers who are "AIRS Certified".

Mark M. continues to say that even with the technological changes within the next five to ten years, the root business of the industry isn't going to change. "Whatever is coming, it won't replace the human connection, assessment, and "gut feel" that a recruiter brings. Recruiters actively reach out to other humans through the phone and in person and convince those individuals to take a look at a new job opportunity. Technology makes business communications and information gathering more streamlined and efficient, but recruiting will always be a contact sport."

Start-Up Your
Business

Because the costs of starting a recruiting business are so low, you probably won't have to seek funding from a bank. All the entrepreneurs interviewed for this book used their own money to start their businesses, including those who rented offices from the get-go. "A few years of successful recruiting gave us the cash to start up," says Tamara L. of herself and her two partners.

If you're low on cash, you could always purchase only the essentials first. You'll already have a phone if you work out of your home, so all you'll really need is a computer to start. You can add extra phone lines, faster internet connections, a workstation, and preprinted stationery as you pick up work.

Assessing the True Costs

We've discussed the requirements of setting up a business and now we need to add up the costs. If you have a decent credit rating, you can be ready to start serving clients with virtually no cash out of pocket—although you'll certainly be on firmer ground if you have some start-up capital. But whether all you have is a credit card or you've got a nice fat savings account ready to invest, opening your doors is only part of the financial picture.

How much does it truly cost to start your own business? Each business is going to be a bit different but Mark M. shares his costs with us. "All my costs, including company logo, web site, incorporating, phones, internet, furniture, office, forms, business cards and letterhead, software, computer, and various miscellaneous costs, I spent around $10K initially and for the next three months lived on another $15K before my first fee. A recruiter starting out needs to include their own personal living expenses for a minimum of three months as part of their start-up costs."

Jeff H. says that the "biggest common mistake is to be undercapitalized. He thought he only needed 120 days to turn a profit. He recommends adding your personal expenses and business expenses and multiplying it by 8 to estimate cash needs. Remember, cash is king!" He continues, "Most entrepreneurs are least prepared about how long the sales cycle takes. The ramp up period is much longer when you're on your own so you need to adequately square away your cash reserves."

The following two worksheets on pages 77 and 78, will help you to compute your initial cash requirements for your business. They list the things you need to consider when determining your start-up costs and include both the one-time initial costs needed to open your doors and the ongoing costs you'll face each month for the first 90 days.

The issue of money has two sides: How much do you need to start and operate, and how much can you expect to take in? Doing this analysis is often extremely difficult for

Beware!
Recent statistics show that the second reason why businesses fail is because of inadequate accounting. Undercapitalization is the main reason.

One-Time Start-Up Costs Worksheet

Start-Up Capital Requirements—One-time Start-Up Expenses		
Start-Up Expenses	**Amount**	**Description**
Advertising and marketing		Your business materials and promotion
Decorating		This is most applicable if you have an office
Deposits		Check with utility companies
Fixtures and equipment		Use actual bids
Insurance		Bids from insurance agents
Lease payments		Fee to be paid before opening office location
Licenses and permits		Check with city or state offices
Miscellaneous		All other
Professional fees		Include CPA, attorney, etc.
Remodeling		Use contractor bids
Rent		Fee to be paid before opening office location
Services		Cleaning, accounting, etc.
Signs		Use contractor bids if opening office location
Supplies		Office, cleaning, etc. supplies
Unanticipated expenses		Include an amount for the unexpected
Other		
Other		
Total Start-Up Costs		Amount of costs before opening

Start-Up Repeating Monthly Expenses Worksheet

Start-Up Capital Requirements—Repeating Monthly Expenses		
Expenses	**Amount**	**Description**
Advertising		
Bank service fees		
Credit card charges		
Dues and subscriptions		
Health insurance		Exclude amount on preceding page
Insurance		Exclude amount on preceding page
Interest		
Lease payments		Exclude amount on preceding page
Loan payments		Principal and interest payments
Office expenses		
Payroll other than owner		
Payroll taxes		
Professional fees		
Rent		Exclude amount on preceding page
Repairs and maintenance		
Sales tax		
Supplies		
Telephone		
Utilities		
Your salary		For at least the first three months
Other		
Total Repeating Costs		
Total Start-Up Costs		Amount from preceding page
Total Cash Needed		

Find more forms for your business at www.entrepreneur.com/formnet.

small-business owners who would rather be in the trenches getting the work done than bound to a desk dealing with tiresome numbers.

Most of the entrepreneurs we talked with used their own personal savings and equipment they already owned to start their businesses. As you're putting together your financial plan, consider these sources of start-up funds:

- *Your own resources.* Do a thorough inventory of your assets. People generally have more assets than they immediately realize. This could include savings accounts, equity in real estate, retirement accounts, vehicles, recreation equipment, collections, and other investments. You may opt to sell assets for cash or use them as collateral for a loan. Take a look, too, at your personal line of credit; most of the equipment you'll need is available through retail stores that accept credit cards. See the Personal Balance Sheet on page 80 to help you determine your net worth.

- *Friends and family.* The logical next step after gathering your own resources is to approach your friends and relatives who believe in you and want to help you succeed. Be cautious with these arrangements; no matter how close you are, present yourself professionally, put everything in writing, and be sure the individuals you approach can afford to take the risk of investing in your business.

- *Partners.* Though most of our entrepreneurs opened their doors by themselves, you may want to consider using the "strength in numbers" principle and look around for someone who may want to team up with you in your venture. You may choose someone who has financial resources and wants to work side-by-side with you in the business. Or you may find someone who has money to invest but no interest in doing the actual work. Be sure to create a written partnership agreement that clearly defines your respective responsibilities and obligations.

- *Government programs.* Take advantage of the abundance of local, state, and federal programs designed to support small businesses. Make your first stop the U.S. Small Business Administration; then investigate various other programs. Women, minorities, and veterans should check out niche financing possibilities designed to help these groups get into business. The business section of your local library is a good place to begin your research.

Naming the Baby

Before you make everything legal and official, you'll need to come up with a name for your business.

Many recruiters simply use their own names: In fact, most of the big recruiting firms use the names of the principals. But other recruiters look for something a little catchier—or a name that's more reflective of their service. It should also be easy to

Personal Balance Sheet

By filling out a personal balance sheet, you will be able to determine your net worth. Finding your net worth early on is an important step in becoming a business owner.

Assets	Totals
Cash and checking	
Savings accounts	
Real estate/home	
Automobiles	
Bonds	
Securities	
Insurance cash values	
Other	
Total Assets A	
Liabilities	**Totals**
Current monthly bills	
Credit card/charge account bills	
Mortgage	
Auto loans	
Finance company loans	
Personal debts	
Other	
Total Liabilities B	
Net Worth (A − B = C) C	
Degree of Indebtedness	
Total Assets A	
Total Liabilities B	
Degree of Indebtedness D	

Source: Entrepreneur Magazine's Start Your Own Business

pronounce and spell—people who can't say your company name may still use you, but they won't refer you to anyone else. You may want to consider not identifying your business as a recruitment firm in the name. Keep in mind that when conducting a search, you'll need to make it past receptionists screening out calls like yours.

The recruiters we spoke to also said that they tried to pick names that weren't already taken by other businesses. And they wanted names that still had an available URL, or the address online.

One entrepreneur we spoke to named her business New Market Partners, a name that reflects the industry she serves, internet businesses. "I had four pages of potential names," she recalls. "Initially, we were thinking New Market Technologies, but when we found that New Market Partners wasn't taken, we grabbed the URL." She adds that they're happy with the name: "We've gotten some good feedback on it."

Another recruiter we interviewed named her business Conrad Cooper Associates. No, there's no one named either Conrad or Cooper associated with the firm. Joseph Conrad and James Cooper are authors—the entrepreneur and her partners liked their work and liked the positive image associated with their names. Besides, the recruiter said, "Incorporating two names is much easier than trying to incorporate Ace Recruiting."

A third entrepreneur wanted to make the point that she conducted business differently because of her fee structure, so she sought out a different name. "We knew we didn't want it to be my name," says the recruiter. "We felt that we do things a little differently. We wanted something that spoke to [the fact] that we were innovative in the way we structure our fees." She chose Search Innovations after finding that other names were already taken.

If you don't want to use your own name for your new recruiting business, use the Naming Your Business Worksheet on page 82 to help you devise one.

Check to see if the name conflicts with any name listed on your state's trademark register. Your state Department of Commerce can either help you or direct you to the correct agency. You should also check with the trademark register maintained by the U.S. Patent and Trademark Office (PTO).

Once the name you've chosen passes these tests, you need to protect it by registering it with the appropriate state agency; again, your state Department of Commerce can help you. Though most executive recruiting services are local operations, if you expect to be doing business on a national level, you should also register the name with the PTO.

▲

Naming Your Business Worksheet

List three ideas based on your specialty. It's best not to be too specific, as many recruiters find that their specialties evolve over time.

1. _____

2. _____

3. _____

List three ideas from names of people you like or admire.

1. _____

2. _____

3. _____

List three ideas using the words "search" or "placement."

1. _____

2. _____

3. _____

Now that you've chosen a few favorites, be sure to do the following for each possibility:

○ Try it out on your friends and family members, especially colleagues in the business. Get their honest opinions.

○ Say it aloud to make sure it's easily understood and pronounced.

○ Listen to it over the phone. You'll be introducing yourself and your business by phone most of the time.

○ Check with your city, county, or state to make sure it hasn't already been taken.

○ Check with internet registries to see if you can use it as your web address.

Are You On a Mission?

At any given moment, most executive recruitment owners have a very clear understanding of the mission of their company. It may not be written down, but they know what they are doing, how and where it's being done, and who their clients are.

If you're a solo operator and want to stay small, it's probably enough for you to keep your mission statement in your head. But if you have employees and want to eventually become a large company, it will help if you are guided by a written mission statement that can be easily communicated to others. A good mission statement helps you—and any employees—stay focused on business goals. If you print it out and place it above your desk, it'll help remind you what your goals are every day.

A mission statement should be short—usually just one sentence and certainly no more than two. A good idea is to cap it at 100 words. Your mission statement doesn't have to be clever or catchy—just accurate.

The mission statement should include your specialty, types of clients, pay structure, and any region you serve. Here are some examples:

- "Our mission is to place corporate attorneys with large businesses in the Dallas area on a contingency basis;" or
- "Our mission is to recruit nursing supervisors for hospitals across the nation. We will work on a retained basis."

Of course, it's not set in stone. If you find your specialty is evolving, or if one sort of pay structure is proving more lucrative, then refine and reprint your mission statement. But always having a mission statement will keep you focused. You will find the Developing Your Mission Statement Worksheet on page 84.

Mission Statement Example

Jeff H.'s company's mission statement is:

"Our mission is to partner with our clients in the search and recruitment of exceptional candidates. We are committed to provide a comfortable environment of trust, integrity, and confidentiality for both our candidates and clients."

Developing Your Mission Statement Worksheet

Use this worksheet to start developing a mission statement for your recruiting business. Your statement should clearly define the following:

○ *Your specialty.* In what industry or field do you expect to make placements?

○ *Your clients.* What sort of clients will need your service?

○ *The pay structure.* Will you work on contingency, retained, hourly, or some sort of combination?

○ *Any region.* If you plan to limit your searches geographically, what is the area you intend to cover?

Mission Statement for

_____

(Name of Your Business)

_____

_____

_____

_____

_____

_____

Making It Official

Many municipalities require all businesses, even homebased ones, to register with the city or county. That may include registering a fictitious business name or obtaining a business license. Check with your city, county, or state to find out what's required.

One of the first decisions you'll need to make about your new business is the legal structure of your company. This is an important decision, and it can affect your financial liability in case someone sues you, the amount of taxes you pay, the degree of ultimate control you have over the company, as well as your ability to raise money, attract investors, and ultimately sell the business.

A sole proprietorship is owned by the proprietor; a partnership is owned by the partners; and a corporation is owned by the shareholders. Another business structure is the limited liability company (LLC), which combines the tax advantages of a sole proprietorship with the liability protection of a corporation. The rules on LLCs vary by state; check with your state's Department of Corporations for the latest requirements.

Most of the entrepreneurs interviewed for this book said they went with a type of corporation because that structure gives them the most protection in case of lawsuits. But while a corporation affords the most protection, be aware that it also requires an attorney to set it up, higher fees, and much more paperwork. However, to take advantage of the protection a corporation offers, you must respect the corporation's identity. That means maintaining the corporation as a separate entity; keeping your corporate and personal funds separate, even if you are the sole shareholder;

Corporate Checklist

If you are going to incorporate, make sure your corporation stays on the right side of the law and pay attention to these guidelines:

❑ Call the Secretary of State each year to check your corporate status.

❑ Put the annual meetings on tickler cards.

❑ Check all contracts to ensure the proper name is used on each. The signature line should read "John Doe, President, XYZ Corp." never just "John Doe."

❑ Never use your name followed by DBA (doing business as) on a contract. Renegotiate any old ones that do.

❑ Before undertaking any activity out of the normal course of business—like purchasing major assets—write a corporate resolution permitting it. Keep all completed forms in the corporate book.

❑ Never use corporate checks for personal debts and vice versa.

❑ Get professional advice about continued retained earnings not needed for immediate operating expenses.

❑ Know in advance what franchise fees are due (if applicable).

Source: Entrepreneur Magazine's Start Your Own Business.

and following your state's rules regarding holding annual meetings and other record-keeping requirements.

Jeff H. says that he incorporated as an S-corporation based on the recommendations of his accountant. However, he has seen that LLCs have become more popular but he feels it was important to incorporate because it helps him stay disciplined with the health of the company because the law requires him to have annual meetings, budgets, etc. It's important to track the finances of the business through budgets, monthly financials, and to have a plan.

> **Quick Quote**
>
> Entrepreneur Jeff H. stresses that it's important to have a good outside accountant and lawyer.

Before you get too far along in setting up your executive search firm, be sure to talk with an accountant and a lawyer. An accountant can help you set up a system for tracking expenses and deductions, figure out your quarterly payments, and generally guide you in keeping your tax payments to a minimum. An attorney can advise you on any possible conflicts with a former employer or future employees, any state laws covering the recruiting business, and issues to be aware of to avoid lawsuits. Both these experts can also give you guidance about the best structure for your recruiting business. A consultation with either of these experts will probably run you about $200. If you decide to incorporate, you're looking at $2,000 to $3,000.

As a business owner, the professional service providers you're likely to need include:

- *Attorney.* You need a lawyer who practices in the area of business law, is honest, and appreciates your patronage. In most parts of the United States, there are many lawyers willing to compete fiercely for the privilege of serving you. Interview several and choose one you feel comfortable with. Be sure to clarify the fee schedule ahead of time, and get your agreement in writing. Keep in mind that good commercial lawyers don't come cheap; if you want good advice, you must be willing to pay for it. Your attorney should review all contracts, leases, letters of intent, and other legal documents before you sign them. He or she can also help you with collecting bad debts and establishing personnel policies and procedures. Of course, if you are unsure of the legal ramifications of any situation, call your attorney immediately.

- *Accountant.* Among your outside advisors, your accountant is likely to have the greatest impact on the success or failure of your business. If you are forming a corporation, your accountant should counsel you on tax issues during start-up. On an ongoing basis, your accountant can help you organize the statistical data concerning your business, assist in charting future actions based on past performance, and advise you on your overall financial strategy regarding purchasing, capital investment, and other matters related to your business goals. A good accountant will also serve as a tax advisor, making sure you are in compliance with all applicable regulations and that you don't overpay any taxes.

- *Insurance agent.* A good independent insurance agent can assist with all aspects of your business insurance, from general liability to employee benefits, and probably even handle your personal lines, as well. Look for an agent who works with a wide range of insurers and understands your particular business. This agent should be willing to explain the details of various types of coverage, consult with you to determine the best coverage, help you understand the degree of risk you are taking, work with you in developing risk-reduction programs, and assist in expediting any claims.

- *Banker.* You need a business bank account and a relationship with a banker. Don't just choose the bank you've always done your personal banking with; it may not be the best bank for your business. Interview several bankers before making a decision on where to place your business. Once your account is opened, maintain a relationship with the banker. Periodically sit down and review your accounts and the services you use to make sure you are getting the package most appropriate for your situation. Ask for advice if you have financial questions or problems. When you need a loan or a bank reference to provide to creditors, the relationship you've established will work in your favor.

- *Consultants.* The consulting industry is booming, and for good reason. Consultants can provide valuable, objective input on all aspects of your business. Consider hiring a business consultant to evaluate your business plan or a marketing consultant to assist you in that area. When you are ready to hire employees, a human resources consultant may help you avoid some costly mistakes. Consulting fees vary widely, depending on the individual's experience, location, and field of expertise.

- *Computer expert.* Your computer is your most valuable physical asset partially because it's probably worth more than your phone, so if you don't know much about computers, find someone to help you select a system and the appropriate software, and who will be available to help you maintain, troubleshoot, and expand your system as you need it.

> **Smart Tip** — *Tip...*
> Not all attorneys are created equal, and you may need more than one. For example, the lawyer who can best guide you in contract negotiations may not be the most effective counsel when it comes to employment issues. Ask about areas of expertise and specialization before retaining a lawyer.

Licenses and Permits

Most cities and counties require business operators to obtain various licenses and permits to comply with local regulations. While you are still in the planning stages, check with your local planning and zoning department or city/county business license department to find out what licenses and permits you will need and how to obtain them. You may need some or all of the following:

Beware!
Find out what type of licenses and permits are required for your business while you're still in the planning stage. You may find out that you can't legally operate the business you're envisioning, so give yourself time to make adjustments to your strategy before you've spent a lot of time and money trying to move in an impossible direction.

- *Occupational license or permit.* This is typically required by the city (or county if you are not within an incorporated city) for just about every business operating within its jurisdiction. License fees are essentially a tax, and the rates vary widely, based on the location and type of business. As part of the application process, the licensing bureau will check to make sure there are no zoning restrictions prohibiting you from operating.

- *State licenses.* Many states require persons engaged in certain occupations to hold licenses or occupational permits. Often, these people must pass state examinations before they can conduct business. It is unlikely that you'll need a state license to operate your business, but it's a good idea to check with your state's occupation licensing entity to be sure.

Business Insurance

Stat Fact
There are more than 2,500 chambers of commerce throughout the country to help you as you start your business. Research yours today.

It takes a lot to start a business—even a small one—so protect your investment with adequate insurance. If you are homebased, don't assume your homeowners' or renters' policy covers your business equipment; chances are, it doesn't. If you're located in a commercial facility, be prepared for your landlord to require proof of certain levels of liability insurance when you sign the lease. And in either case, you need coverage for your equipment, supplies, clients' materials, and other valuables.

Smart Tip

Tip...

Sit down with your insurance agent every year and review your insurance needs. As your company grows, they are sure to change. Also, insurance companies are always developing new products to meet the needs of the growing small-business market, and it's possible one of these new policies is appropriate for you.

A smart approach to insurance is to find an agent who works with other professional services businesses. The agent should be willing to help you analyze your needs, evaluate the risks you're willing to accept, and the risks you need to insure against, and work with you to keep your insurance costs down.

Typically, homebased businesses will want to make sure their equipment is insured against theft and damage by a covered peril, such as fire or flood, and that they have some liability protection if someone (either a client or an employee) is injured on their property. In most cases, one of the new insurance products designed for homebased businesses will provide sufficient coverage. Also, if you use your vehicle for business, be sure it is adequately covered.

If you opt for a commercial location, your landlord will probably require certain levels of general liability coverage as part of the terms of your lease. You'll also want to cover your supplies, equipment, and fixtures. Once your business is up and running, consider business interruption insurance to replace lost revenue and cover related costs if you are ever unable to operate due to covered circumstances.

The insurance industry is responding to the special needs of small businesses by developing affordable products that provide coverage on equipment, liability, and even loss of income.

You will need a lawyer and an accountant to consult with you on your insurance needs. However, to help you plan, the Business Insurance Planning Worksheeet on page 90 is a short list of business insurance types that you may want to ask if you need.

Smart Tip

Tip...

When you purchase insurance on your equipment, ask what documentation the insurance company requires before you have to file a claim. That way, you'll be sure to maintain appropriate records, and the claims process will be easier if it is ever necessary.

For example, Jeff H. was advised by his accountant and lawyer that he didn't need Errors and Omissions Insurance for his business, but other entrepreneurs have preferred to carry it.

Business Insurance Planning Worksheet

Types of Insurance	Required? (y/n)	Cost per Payment	Annual Cost
1. General Liability Insurance			
2. Errors and Omissions Liability Insurance			
3. Automotive Liability Insurance			
4. Fire and Theft Insurance			
5. Business Interruption Insurance			
6. Overhead Expense Insurance			
7. Personal Disability			
8. Key-Employee Insurance			
9. Shareholders' or Partners' Insurance			
10. Credit Extension Insurance			
11. Term Life Insurance			
12. Health Insurance			
13. Group Insurance			
14. Workers' Compensation Insurance			
15. Profit Insurance			
16. Money and Securities Insurance			
17. Power Interruption			
18. Fidelity Bonds			
19. Title Insurance			
20. Water Damage Insurance			
Total Annual Cost		$	$

Find more forms for your business at www.entrepreneur.com/formnet.

9

The
Contract

Before you take on your first assignment, you'll need to sign a contract with your client. But before you do that, you should establish what payment method you want to request. In the recruiting industry, there is a distinction between contingency recruiters and retained recruiters—not only in how they are paid but also in how they approach the job.

You'll also want to decide whether to offer a guarantee for your placements. You can always negotiate individual assignments with clients, but you'll be less vulnerable—and you'll appear more professional—if you have set terms.

Get It in Writing

Let's look at a scenario: you have a client looking for a few good candidates and luckily for you, you've found one for them. The client hasn't signed anything yet and you are about to tell them the candidate's name and contact information? Hold on there. They haven't signed a contract promising that they will pay you a dime if they hire your candidate. Don't show your cards or you will see that candidate waltz into that job and leave you with nothing. There goes all your work with no pay.

Don't let your eagerness keep you from covering your bases or be afraid of asking for a signature. If they aren't willing to put your verbal agreement in writing, then maybe this isn't the client for you.

Quoting from your Fee Schedule (a recruiter's price sheet) is not the same thing as a Fee Agreement. Just because they say OK to what you have on a pricing sheet doesn't mean that they have agreed to pay you. Have your fees, terms, and conditions all in writing once you and the client have agreed upon them together and have it signed by an authorized representative of the company. Don't make it any longer than a page and make sure you're professional. Even then, this might not be legally enforceable; but your lawyer can review those issues with you, and at least it will make collecting payment easier since both parties understand the agreement. By doing this before you release the candidate's information you have done the following::

- *Clarified.* If there was any confusion or questions, then this is the time to work them out. Make it simple and confirm that you're both on the same page.

> **Smart Tip** _Tip..._
>
> If you're hoping to move into retained searches, approach a steady client with the proposition. Tell them that if they guarantee payment, you can do a better job of selecting and screening candidates. If they're happy with your work so far, they may go for it.

- *Improved image.* You have probably gotten some points for professionalism. Although most recruiters work on the honor system, it shows you're not an amateur. New recruiters tend to give away their services and shy away from the confrontation of asking for a contract.

- *Qualified.* You now know that you have a serious client. If the client isn't willing to sign the contract, then they probably weren't serious about hiring or worse, paying you.

- *Established*. You have built a relationship by setting boundaries. This is the groundwork necessary to make a partnership last.

Now let's look at what that contract structure may be and how to agree to a contract.

Contingency vs. Retained Fees

Recruiters are paid a fairly standard rate: between one-quarter and one-third of the final, agreed-upon annual salary of the candidate who accepts the position. But while the rate is pretty standard, the payment method can be either retained, contingency, or a combination of the two.

The long-term success and profitability of a recruiting business has little to do with the form of payment it uses. But recruiters who want to move into retained searches frequently find that they need to start out with contingency assignments before they can build up a reputation and loyal client base that's willing to pay on a retained basis.

The recruiters interviewed for this book say that contingency and retained jobs call for very different approaches. Contingency recruiters are focused on placing people, while retained recruiters act more as consultants to their clients. You may find that your personality suits one approach better than the other: If you like to focus on a few larger projects and work closely with clients, retained recruiting may be a good goal. On the other hand, if you like to juggle a number of projects at once and have little interest in mentoring clients, it might be best to stick with contingency.

Donna K., who runs her own one-person recruiting business in New York City, says she likes the freedom and flexibility of contingency work. "I can work on any number of jobs at a time," she says, adding that she often has about 30 positions she's trying to fill at once. "Because I work on contingency, if I'm working a job and I find out that it's an exceptionally difficult position to fill, I can choose to not work that hard on it."

Beware!
While candidates rarely leave their posts before the guarantee period is up, a few of the recruiters interviewed for this book said that they've had to refund money. However, it happened only once during their careers.

On the other hand, Vivian K. in Philadelphia started her firm as a retained business, and never wanted to do contingency. "It's a different business in my opinion," she says. "I view retained as very client-focused and project-focused, and I view contingency as very candidate-focused."

Contingency and retained aren't the only options. Many recruiting firms ask for a combination, receiving some money up front to start the search, then the rest when the candidate is

Payment Pathways

Your level of experience, your relationship with clients, and your work style will determine whether you decide to work on contingency or retainer. But you don't necessarily have to choose one payment method: You may find that certain clients work best in a contingency arrangement, others with a retainer agreement. Below are some of the advantages and disadvantages of both payment methods.

CONTINGENCY

Advantages

- ○ It's easier to get assignments from clients.
- ○ You can drop assignments that are difficult to fill.
- ○ You're under no obligation to work with a client if the client turns out to be difficult.

Disadvantages

- ○ There's no guarantee you'll be paid for your time.
- ○ You're often competing with other recruiters.
- ○ You must juggle many assignments at once because you'll fill only a fraction of your assignments.

RETAINED

Advantages

- ○ You're guaranteed payment for your time.
- ○ You can focus on fewer assignments and do a more thorough job.
- ○ Clients give you more attention since you're the only recruiter on the job.

Disadvantages

- ○ It's more difficult to get assignments from clients.
- ○ You're guaranteeing you'll fill a position.
- ○ You're more likely to get into disputes with clients over background checks and choice of candidates.

hired. You can also ask for one-third upfront, one-third when you present three appropriate candidates, and the rest upon hiring. Any varieties of combinations work, as long as both you and the client are happy with the arrangement.

Tamara L., who started a search firm in San Mateo, California, says her firm usually asks for $5,000 to $10,000 up front, then the remainder when an offer is made. The initial payment ensures her firm that the client will hire one of the candidates her firm selects, whereas the final payment ensures the client that her firm will provide candidates quickly. But Tamara adds that her firm will also do contingency or retained searches, depending on how the client wants to operate.

Comes with a Guarantee

Most recruiters guarantee that their candidates will stay on the job for a certain length of time, usually between 30 days and one year. If the candidate leaves before the guarantee period is up, the recruiter either needs to refund the money or perform another search free of charge. Offering a guarantee ensures your clients that you're making an effort to find someone who'll stick, not just anyone who can fill the job. Typically, the higher up the position is in the corporate structure, the longer the guarantee period.

Not all recruiters like to make guarantees. Ken C., the recruiter in Panama City Beach, Florida, says he avoids offering guarantee periods. "I don't hire anybody," he says. "The client is the one who hires them. If someone doesn't last very long, that sounds like a management problem to me." When a client presses him to offer a guarantee period, he says, he'll give them a year. But, he adds, "I can't recall anyone I've put in a company leaving and someone reminding me that I have to replace them."

Sign on the Dotted Line

Once you and your client have agreed to the payment, the pay schedule, and any guarantee period, put it down on paper. Draw up a standard contract and have your lawyer review it. Doing this can save many a headache—and possibly a court battle—later on.

The contract should include the following information:

- *The fee you'll receive.* State what percentage of the candidate's annual salary you will receive (usually between 25 and 33 percent). This is the salary that the company and the candidate negotiate, not as the job is listed. Some recruiters also ask for a percentage of hiring bonuses and the value of any fringe benefits such as the use of company cars and memberships in country clubs.

- *When the client will pay you the fee.* If it's contingency work, this will be after your candidate accepts the position. If it's retainer work, you need to spell out what percentage of your fee you want beforehand. For example, retained recruiters may ask for 30 percent of the expected annual salary up front, 30 percent after a month, 30 percent after two months, then the rest upon a candidate's acceptance of the job.

Beware!
A contract needn't be signed and dated to be valid. Agreement to an arrangement can be spoken or made through emails. It can also be implicit, such as when a client sends you a check. Unsigned agreements can hold up in a court of law, so be careful what you agree to, even if you haven't placed your John Hancock on a dotted line.

- *Your guarantee period.* State your guarantee period and what you'll do if the candidate leaves before the period is over. If you'll refund the money, say so. If you'll conduct a new search, say that. If you want your expenses paid for the second search, make sure to include that in the contract.

The contract may also include:

- *Periodic updates of your work.* If you've agreed to keep your client up to date on your search, put this in your contract. Manny A., the recruiter in Chicago, says that he includes a statement that he will give his clients weekly updates on his progress.

- *A "hands-off" policy on company employees.* In the recruiting industry, it's understood that you won't approach any employees of a client company to see if they're interested in positions with other companies. But some clients may prefer to have this noted in the contract. You can say you'll stay away from employees for one or two years after you've made a placement with the company.

- *A disclaimer on reference checks.* You'll want to check out a candidate's background for your own purposes, but to cover yourself, it's a good idea to include a disclaimer. The disclaimer basically states that you've conducted reference checks for your own information, but that the client also agrees to verify the information. This way, you may be able to avoid a lawsuit if it turns out that a candidate has misrepresented himself or herself (it happens more frequently than you might imagine) and you didn't catch it.

Sample Contingency and Retainer Contracts are provided on pages 97 and 98.

Contingency Contract

Placement Pals
345 Hiring Way
Job City, RI 55555

January 31, 20xx

Paul Personnel
Human Resources Manager
Wizard Widgets Inc.
9876 Manufacturing Way
Employment, AL 44444

Dear Paul,

This letter signifies our agreement regarding recruitment for the engineer position.

Placement Pals shall be paid for all referrals that result in a hire with Wizard Widgets regardless of any agreements Wizard Widgets has entered into with other recruiters. Placement Pals will receive 30 percent of the employee's annual salary once the employee has accepted the position. If the employee leaves the position within 60 days of starting, Placement Pals will refund its placement fee.

Placement Pals makes reference and background checks for its own purposes but does not verify any claims made by the candidates. Wizard Widgets agrees to independently check any personal, employment, or educational representations made by the candidate.

Once Placement Pals makes a referral that results in a hire, Placement Pals agrees not to approach any employee of Wizard Widgets regarding positions in other companies for a period of one year.

Paul Personnel, Wizard Widgets	Rena Recruiter, Placement Pals

▲

Retainer Contract

Placement Pals
345 Hiring Way
Job City, RI 55555

January 31, 20xx

Paul Personnel
Human Resources Manager
Wizard Widgets Inc.
9876 Manufacturing Way
Employment, AL 44444

Dear Paul,

This letter signifies our agreement regarding recruitment for the engineer position.

Placement Pals shall be paid a total of 30 percent of the final negotiated annual salary, including any hiring bonuses and the value of club memberships and car use. Wizard Widgets will pay 10 percent of the expected annual salary, or $7,000 immediately. One month from this date, Placement Pals shall be paid another 10 percent, or $7,000. Two months from this date, Placement Pals shall receive 5 percent, or $3,500. Upon completion of the hire, Placement Pals shall receive the remaining 5 percent, or $3,500, contingent on the final negotiated annual salary.

If a placement is made before two months, Placement Pals shall receive the entire 30 percent upon hire. Placement Pals agrees to make weekly reports regarding the search for appropriate candidates.

If the employee leaves the company for any reason before one year after the date of hire, Placement Pals will conduct another search free of charge. Once Placement Pals makes a referral that results in a hire, Placement Pals agrees not to approach any employee of Wizard Widgets regarding positions in other companies for a period of one year.

Paul Personnel, Wizard Widgets	Rena Recruiter, Placement Pals

Keep Your Hands Off

Before we start talking about finding candidates, we must make it very clear that client companies are always hands off. You must never try to recruit a candidate from any company that hires you to fill positions. If you do, you will lose that client forever, and that client will spread the word about you within your specialty. Trust us—you'll have an awfully tough time finding new job orders.

Some recruiters write a hands-off policy into their contracts with their clients, others say it's not necessary. "Even if it's not written in, it's such an unwritten rule," says Tamara L. It's just understood within the recruiting industry that this is something you never do. In hiring you, the client has given you access to its organizational chart and its employees, and to recruit from that client would violate that privilege.

Essential Attributes of a Recruiter

The Association of Executive Search Consultants (AESC) published a report based on a survey of client corporations. The seven attributes of an executive search firm they found most critical were:

○ Confidential handling of information exchanged during a search assignment

○ Clear understanding of the company culture, open position, and the required background and experience and competencies that are reflected in a position description

○ Market intelligence on the availability of candidates and comparative assessment of their compensation levels and as well as impression the client's company in the market

○ Comprehensive knowledge of the industry in which they specialize and conduct the search

○ Policy of not sourcing from the client firm for an allocated amount of time after the search

○ Close consultation with key decision makers during the assessment of needs and process of the search assignment

○ Guarantee that a candidate will be provided to replace a placement that leaves before a prescribed period of time at no additional cost

For more information, go to www.aesc.org.

However, if candidates resign from a client company, then approach a recruiter to help them find new positions, they're free game. Tamara says her firm has the candidate sign a waiver saying the recruiters did not recruit the candidate in any way, just in case a client company objects.

The hands-off policy is not permanent. Some of our entrepreneurs say they'll recruit from a previous client if they haven't received any job orders from those clients within one or two years.

The
Search

The real business of executive recruiting is the search, so let's look at defining the job you hope to fill, then finding names of candidates—through networking, the internet, and cold calling.

What's the Job?

You can't start looking for a candidate until you have a complete and accurate job description. If a client gives you a vague description of the position it wants you to fill, you need to ask a number of questions until you're clear about the qualifications. To whom will the employee report? What skills are needed? Will this be a job that requires interpersonal skills? Will this person be managing others? Does the employee need to speak any foreign languages or know certain computer programming languages? If you're familiar with the field in which you're searching, you'll be more prepared to ask the right questions to better define the job.

Entrepreneur Mark M. says that "candidate control is important but so is client control. About 90 percent of all the client control you will have will be because you took a good job order. Getting the job order is more than just writing down the job specs. You should also consult the client on the best way to recruit candidates and get information on the company culture. The time you spend on this aspect of the search will help determine how well you perform for your client."

Beware!
If a client is cagey about the job specs, proceed with caution. Sometimes companies will ask recruiters to find candidates just to fill their resume drawer in case something comes up. Don't search unless everything about the job is nailed down.

"There are some clients who give you every amount of detail possible," says Tamara L., who runs a search firm in San Mateo, California. "Other ones say 'We need software engineers and they need to know Java.' When it's vague, we ask them more details, such as what sort of interpersonal skills are needed."

But don't just get a job description from the human resources person. If you dig a little deeper, you'll get a much better idea of what the job entails, and you'll be in a better position to make a good match. Talk to the person leaving the position, the supervisor the new employee will report to, the subordinates who will report to the new employee, and any other co-workers.

Be sure to acquire at least the following:

- The location of the job
- The salary range
- Why there's a vacancy
- The title of the position
- The responsibilities
- Educational requirements
- Experience requirements

- Appropriate personality characteristics

Also find out as much as you can about the company: What services or products does it sell? How long has it been around? What's the culture like? What are the company's future goals? How profitable is it? You want to have a good picture of the company so you and the candidates will know whether it'll be a good fit for them. Say a candidate tells you "I can't work past 5," and you know that no one at the company ever leaves before 6:30 P.M. In that case, it may not be worth your while to try to get the candidate an interview. In short, the more you know about the position and the company, the less time you'll waste searching for and talking with candidates who aren't appropriate.

One thing that recruiters notoriously forget to ask is "why is the position open?" When you relay the opportunity to the candidate you want to say what the drama or desired outcome will be so that you have a story to tell and describe how the company hopes to be "rescued" from this problem. What does the company's best case scenario?

You don't just want keywords and bullet points. They don't help you to:

- Understand the problem
- Prioritize skill sets (remember, they are describing the "unicorn" candidate)
- Decide which candidates are most qualified
- Propose alternate candidates that may be lacking some keywords
- Add to your credibility

Your goal is to tell a story and cast a candidate to play the role. What will the candidate's mission be? Their goal? Are they ensuring the safety of employees in an

On the Right Path

A detailed job description is only part of the information you want from your client. Also be sure to ask whether the client is willing to pay relocation costs. If not, you know you need to focus your search on candidates working in the same metropolitan area. You may be able to find clients from outside the area who are interested in moving, but your best bets will be right where the client is.

Ask your clients if they have any ideas on where you could find the best candidates. Your client may also have ideas about which companies it would like its candidates to have in their background. Certain businesses have good reputations for training their employees well, and your client may want to take advantage of that. Other companies may be very similar to your client's, so candidates from those companies would fit well within the organization.

industry? Are they leading the sales effort for an exciting new national product? You can attract better candidates if you get them interested in the job, and a boring job description isn't going to get their attention.

Write up a job description and send it to your client before you start your search to make sure you're all on the same page. You'll also use this description to find appropriate candidates.

Make the Job Description Your Tool

When creating a job description, always use appealing language to promote the position versus merely listing a roster of skills and duties. Read your description as if you are the potential candidate. Does it employ friendly, image-rich language such as strong, team, challenged, casual, hottest, and future? These words help create a description that makes it easy for the job seeker to imagine herself in the position. It makes her want to know more about the company because it sounds like a fun, interesting place to work.

Ineffective descriptions are just a laundry list of basic data; it does little to market the job or the company. It doesn't reach out with enticing language—the burden is on the job seeker to try to picture himself or herself doing that job at that company. Neglecting to sell the position by writing an effective posting is a missed marketing opportunity. Your goal is to help highly qualified applicants picture themselves performing this job with your client.

Don't waste the potential candidate's time discussing the history of the company or the details of the job. You are not a classified ad so don't sound like you're reading the job description straight from the newspaper. Instead, introduce yourself and mention WHY the company is hiring. You are selling the NEED or result, not the job description. Who gets excited about task descriptions? You want them to see themselves in the job before you even ask if they might be interested.

For example, say that you represent a growing company that is opening a new product division and they need an experienced sales manager to hire and develop a national sales team. When you ask if they are possibly interested in an opportunity like that, you are more likely to get a "yes" than if you listed the company's mission statement and tasks.

For example, as discussed previously, with active candidates, some are so specialized in

Smart Tip

Tip...

Be professional and try to build a relationship on every call. Most people you talk to when looking for candidates aren't going to be looking for a job. However, they almost always know someone they can refer. Getting that referral is much easier when they already trust you.

their skill sets that there are so few of them in the market that they sometimes have the jobs come to them. Those are the candidates that you need to call and ask what they are looking for in their next job and keep them on file so you know where to find them when a job order that fits their description comes across your desk.

Some other candidates are industry-specific, and they want to know about a job you have now. If you don't have a job that might fit their skills, then you probably won't get an ideal response. Prep for these calls with a "sell" about the current opportunity.

Don't forget to always ask for referrals! If they aren't in the market for a move, they may know someone who would be interested.

Sourcing for Candidates

All the recruiters interviewed for this book said they use every possible channel to get lists of candidates. "I use the internet, I will run ads occasionally, certainly word-of-mouth, certainly cold calling, networking, you name it," says Donna K. in New York City.

"There are many, many ways to find candidates," adds Ken C. in Panama City Beach, Florida. "I'll take qualified candidates from any source at all—I don't care if they show up at my door. I take candidates from business schools, executive networking groups, and online."

Many recruiters complain that it's hard to find quality candidates. That may be the case if you don't know where to look. Top performers are your ideal candidates and it is common knowledge that most of them have common tendencies and characteristics. Here are just a few suggestions to brainstorm a candidate profile:

Media

- What newspapers, magazines, trade journals, professional publications and newsletters do they read?
- In what listservs, e-mail newsletters, and web sites do they belong or contribute to?

Events

- What professional conferences would they regularly attend?
- What self-development or professional seminars do they attend?
- What type of social, nonprofit, or community events do they attend?
- Do they ever attend career-building or networking events?

Organizations

- Of what professional organizations are they a member?
- To what social or community organizations do they belong?
- To which university or alumni associations do they belong?

Miscellaneous

- Are there other events in the industry that they might attend?
- To what networking sites do they belong?
- Is there a current socioeconomic effort in your community they might be supporting?
- What charity events do they attend or support?

The recruiters add that none of these methods work any better than others—good candidates come from all sources. The best place to start is with your own contacts. Let's say you're recruiting for the HMO project director position in our examples: Start calling friends, acquaintances, and all your business contacts in the health-care business, and ask them if they know someone who might be good for the position. Compile a list of names of people to call. Record these potential candidates in your database, along with their contact information and the name of the person who recommended them to you.

You may also know the names of some people from trade journals or association meetings. "I'll hear a name in my networking or my travels, and maybe their title is appropriate," says Donna K. Put these people on your list of potential candidates as well.

You can also find names of people by researching your client's competition. Head to the library and learn the Standard Industry Classification (SIC) code of your client company, and then find other companies with the same SIC code. In our HMO example, you'll be looking for other health-care organizations in your area. The client may also have given you a list of companies from which they'd like you to recruit.

But remember that good candidates may come from other types of organizations as well. In our example, a qualified candidate may hail from the educational or government sector. Find out the names of school districts and social service agencies, such as the city or state department of public health. Try to think of the types of companies that would have candidates with appropriate experience.

Another source of names may be acquired from association listings. Some industry associations publish member lists. Try an online search and ask your contacts in the field for the names of associations. Alumni associations for graduate schools may also be a good source of names. For our HMO position, for example, we could try lists from schools or departments that give degrees in public health.

As you might imagine, the internet is an indispensable tool for recruiters. Several of our entrepreneurs look at job boards such as Headhunter.net and Monster.com, where job seekers post their resumes. You can also look at newsgroups and discussion forums where your candidates might hang out. You might find a discussion forum for directors of public health projects, for example. Try a newsgroup search engine to find newsgroups in your field.

But other recruiters say they don't spend a lot of time searching online. "By the time our clients get to us, a lot of them have done the internet route," says Vivian K., the recruiter out of Philadelphia. "They've either advertised on Monster, or they've had someone comb the internet to find people." She adds that her clients hire her to find the candidates who aren't easily accessible.

Tamara L. says that she uses the internet to find people, but adds that she can't spend all day on the computer. "If you go completely internet, that's a waste of your time," she says. "On the other hand if you don't use it, you're ignoring a great resource."

Why don't you want to focus only on candidates available online? There are more than just three reasons, but many recruiters sum it up this way:

- *Scarcity*. There is a shortage of candidates with specialized or esoteric skills that are willing to post online. Why should they? There aren't many people that can do what they do so they are waiting to be sought out. Candidates like these are typically accustomed to jobs coming to them versus candidates with common skills need to seek positions that can be easily filled by someone else.

- *Competition*. If the candidate is actively searching, they probably have numerous opportunities. It's a waste of your time to compete with your candidates and other recruiters.

- *Quality*. Whether it's true or not, there is a perception by hiring managers that actively searching candidates are less desirable than the candidates who aren't looking to make a move since the passive ones must be super stars at their current jobs. Active candidates get labeled as disloyal, unemployable, or job-hoppers.

Sourcing online can result in numerous resumes, but you would be naïve to think that being able to download one means that you have a serious candidate. Until you dedicate your efforts to confirm that is the case, you need to focus on transforming these leads into candidates before the next recruiter does.

Entrepreneur Jeff H. says that "In recent years, the internet and job boards have become widely used for both sourcing candidates and as a means for candidates to find opportunities. These web sites definitely have a place, but once again you only identify the people in the workforce who are unemployed or, for whatever reason, are looking for a job. Probably the biggest issue and hidden cost to these job boards are the hundreds of resumes of totally unrelated, unqualified candidates that you have to sift through to find someone who comes remotely close to the qualifications necessary for the position. If you are lucky enough to find someone after all of this, you still miss access to the 60 percent of the workforce that is happy, successful, being promoted, and not considering a change in employment at this time. Once again, the only way to find those candidates is by engaging a professional recruiter who has the access and reputation to entice these candidates into considering a new opportunity."

Even those recruiters who don't search online to find candidates say that they find it an invaluable resource for researching industries and businesses. "We do what we call industry research," says Vivian K. "We get to know everything about the industry—the awards, conferences—everything that has to do with the particular industry at hand."

Finally, some recruiters say they'll advertise for a position. Of course, if your client has already tried this approach, you're probably wasting your time and money. Donna K. says she advertises occasionally for jobs in local newspapers, internet job boards, and trade magazines.

Mark M. recommended the Sample Candidate Application on page 109 as a good generic job search application. If there is any additional information that you would like to have on file about the candidate, be sure to add it to this template. Remember, the information you ask here will save you from needing to ask in an interview. Add your company logo to all of your materials and include your contact information.

Getting Past the Gatekeeper

Now that you have a list of source companies where you believe you have potential candidates, here's the hard part. You'll need to find the names of people within those companies who might be interested in applying for your position. Sometimes this will be easy: A company may list its employees on its web site or in its annual report. Or, if it's a publication, it'll list the contributors to the publication in its masthead.

Other times, you'll have to call and try to find out. Many receptionists are wary of calls from recruiters, so they may be reluctant to patch you through unless you give specific names. And if you start asking questions like, "Who in your organization has experience in directing public health projects?" they'll be on to you in one second, and the line will be dead in two.

> **Bright Idea**
> Several firms offer subscriptions to resume databases and other search services. For a hefty annual fee (between $500 and $2,500), you can use the database to search for candidates or research companies more quickly than you can using regular search engines. Some popular services are AIRS (www.airsdirectory.com) and Recruiterlink.com.

Sample Candidate Application

Instructions: Please complete all spaces in BLACK pen.

Date of Application		Interview Availability		
Last Name, First, MI		Residence Phone	Business Phone	Mobile Phone
Home Address City, State Zip		[ ] Own home [ ] Rent	No. Years in Present Location	No. Years in the Community
Spouse's Name	Spouse's Occupation Name of Company and Phone		[ ] Referred / Called By	
Contact in Emergency (Not Spouse) City		Phone	Professional Memberships, Licenses	

Education	Name of School	Location	From	To	Graduate?	Degree Title	Major or Major Subjects
College or University							
College or University							
Others: Graduate School, Military, Technical, Trade							

References	Occupation	Company	Telephone	Address City

Sample Candidate Application, continued

Position Desired

A.	B.	Foreign Languages (fluent)	[ ] U.S. Citizen [ ] Have Resume [ ] Not U.S. Citizen [ ] Don't Have Resume [ ] Eligible to Work [ ] Will Make Resume [ ] Can you begin ASAP? [ ] If No, When?

Work History	Present or Last Position	Prior Position	Position Before Prior
Dates Employed	From To	From To	From To
Company Name			
Company Address			
Supervisor Name & Title			
	Company Phone	Company Phone	Company Phone
	Supervisor's Phone	Supervisor's Phone	Supervisor's Phone
Base Salary (Annual)	Now $ Start $	Now $ Start $	Now $ Start $
Additional	Now $ Start $	Now $ Start $	Now $ Start $
Total	Now $ Start $	Now $ Start $	Now $ Start $

Your Title

Please list the exact duties you perform:

Sample Candidate Application, continued

Company Product or Service									
$ Volume in Millions	Co.	This Div.	This Plant	Co.	This Div.	This Plant	Co.	This Div.	This Plant
No. of Employees	Total Here	This Dept	You Sup	Total Here	This Dept	You Sup	Total Here	This Dept	You Sup
Two of Your Competitors	1 2			1 2			1 2		
Reason for Leaving									

The best approach is to try to be direct, but say as little as possible. Give your name and your firm's name (unless it's Recruiters Are Us, it won't necessarily give you away), and ask to speak with someone in charge of public health projects. You may get through; if not, try again later, as someone else might answer the phone.

If you're having a difficult time breaking into an organization, go back to your contacts and see if anyone knows someone within that company. Your contact may not be in the right department, but you may get directed to the right department. Persistence is the key to compiling a list of potential candidates' names.

Some entrepreneurs interviewed for this book skip this whole process and instead hire search researchers.

11

Setting the
Stage

We've gone over how to source candidates. Now let's go over how to prepare your scripts, prequalifying, screening, and getting referrals.

The Script of the Matter

Bright Idea

Gary Stauble, a principal consultant for The Recruiting Lab, has recommended some of his favorite scripts to improve your effectiveness with each call. Check them out online at www.therecruitinglab.com. To see some of his articles, go to www.net-temps.com under Recruiter News.

Now you have a list of names, but before you pick up the phone to contact your potential candidates, prepare yourself for what you're going to say. If you haven't had much or any hands-on experience in executive recruiting, you could be drooling over the idea of some pre-made scripts to get you over the newbie jitters. However, as helpful as scripts are, they can also be constrictive and you can sound robotic if you cling to them for support. They are great training wheels if you use them properly.

If you want to take a stab at writing your own scripts, make sure to make them interesting. Remember that if you don't get their attention within your first few sentences, the call is already over.

If you need some help, scripts that can be used as templates are available through many recruiting networking sites, training seminars, and industry books such as the ones listed in the Appendix.

One word of advice, despite whichever option you choose, developing your own script or using a sample, don't use the same script on every call. Quality passive candidates aren't going to listen to a cookie-cutter, overly-rehearsed and impersonal sales pitch. If they turn you down, it may not be just because of your script, but you can minimize the rejections if you customize each call to the person you are calling.

Don't treat your script like an English class essay that needs to be beautifully-crafted and masterfully delivered. It is your tool and you need it to serve you in whatever way might be best. No two candidates are alike, so neither should your scripts.

Scripts are important and they are constantly changing pieces of art that you need to mold to each call. Remember that this is a people-based business and although you're working with large salaries and careers, it's also an emotion-based business. You should recognize that although each step is part of a process, it's truly just a path to build relationships. Even though you might only spend a few minutes on

Smart Tip

Tip...

Run your scripts by a colleague: Have him or her listen to you on the phone and give honest criticism of your tone and voice. If you have a tendency to speak too loudly or too quickly, put a note on your phone reminding you to lower the volume or slow down.

the phone with the potential candidate, you want them to still trust and respect you. Think about that objective when working on your scripts.

Working the Phone

You want to sell the candidate on the job without sounding too much like you're trying to sell. Write down two scripts, one for voicemail and one for a live contact. Also get out your job description and questionnaire.

"You go in and talk about the company, the job, and career opportunity," says Larry D., the franchisee in Huntersville, North Carolina. "You try to paint a good picture so the candidate will say 'Wow, that does sound good.' And if they're not interested, they'll refer you to a friend."

Don't give the name of the client at this point. If you're working on a contingency basis, you don't want the candidate contacting the client on his or her own—or telling friends about the job. Then you'll be out a commission. Even if you're working on a retained job, it's best to keep the client's name quiet for a while in case the company prefers to keep a low profile.

Chances are good that you'll have to leave a message, either with a receptionist or a machine. An example of a voice message for the project director job would be: "I'm

You Never Know

Call every name on your list, even if you doubt the person will help or you're feeling nervous because you don't have a referral. It's often more difficult to make cold calls, but these can be just as productive.

Donna K., the recruiter in New York City, says she doesn't shy away from calling people out of the blue: "Sometimes you get lucky—you make a cold call and say 'I'm not sure whether you're looking, but I thought I'd just call and introduce myself,' and they say 'Perfect timing. I just decided last night to put myself on the market.' You never know."

Making cold calls also introduces you to new people and expands your list of contacts. The next time you call, you won't be cold calling. Lukewarm calling, maybe, but now you have someone you can refer to when you need help.

Beware!

Never leave a voice-mail message saying that you're calling because your contact is a possible candidate for a position you're trying to fill. There's always the chance that an assistant or even a supervisor could be screening messages. Instead, say you're calling to see if they know someone who might be appropriate for the job.

Rena Recruiter calling on behalf of a large, growing health-care organization. We're looking for a project director to manage an educational program for teenagers. I'm calling to see if you have any thoughts or suggestions on who might fit this position." Then, of course, give your phone number.

When your contacts call back, or if you catch someone live, you can expand your pitch a little more: "We're looking for someone who has experience directing projects in health care, fundraising, and working with the educational system. Is there anyone you could recommend for this opportunity?"

Asking them if they know someone lets them bow out gracefully if they don't want the job themselves or if they don't fit the criteria. If they're interested, they'll say so. If they're not, they can perhaps give you names of some colleagues who are.

Once you find someone who's interested, ask if this is a good time to talk. (It'll be awfully hard for your candidate to be at all candid if the boss is standing in the doorway.) If it's not a good time, ask if you can call at home or on a cell phone after work.

When you have his or her full attention, mention that you've heard good things about him or her (everyone loves flattery), but you don't have all the details on his or her background. Then refer to your questionnaire: If he or she say 'Yes' to every question, you have a possible match. Ask him or her to send you a resume.

If candidates don't fit the qualifications, don't lead them on. Explain that the client is looking for someone with more experience in health care or with grant writing. Add that their qualifications are otherwise impressive and that you'll contact them if you're filling a position that fits them more closely. You never know when you'll need their help again, so you want to be straightforward but polite.

By the end of this process, you'll have a pile of resumes from candidates who come near to fitting the qualifications. The next step will be interviewing, checking references, and presenting them to the client.

It's important to plan and track your calls for the day. The Phone Log on page 117 is a sample template to track your daily calls.

Smart Tip

Tip...

If you leave a message and haven't heard back within a week, call again. The message might have been lost, or your contact may have meant to call but forgot. If you leave two messages and you don't hear back, don't call again. This person isn't interested in helping you, and calling a third time would only be harassment.

Phone Log

Today's Phone Calls

Name   Date

Location

Call	Item	Result	Reschedule
Name: Company: Phone:			
Name: Company: Phone:			
Name: Company: Phone:			
Name: Company: Phone:			
Name: Company: Phone:			
Name: Company: Phone:			
Name: Company: Phone:			
NOTES			

Find more forms for your business at www.entrepreneur.com/formnet.

Overcoming Objections

Every type of sale comes with objections, and if you balk at each one then you have less of a chance at closing the deal. Instead, use rebuttals, stories and examples to help address the issues that are causing the other party to say "no".

If you find that you're failing to perform a good sales job at certain points in the search and placement process, it may be helpful to track the trends. If, for example, you're finding lots of candidates, but you're not getting them to agree to an interview, you'll need to sell the job better. And part of doing that is responding to their concerns.

Make a list of your most common objections and you'll realize that there aren't all that many. Maybe a client won't hire you because you don't have experience in the industry or they already have a recruiter. Maybe the client should consider using you despite your inexperience in the industry because you can offer a fresh perspective.

After each objection, form an appropriate rebuttal to address each one and keep them handy so you can refer to them when you're on the phone. Say the position you're trying to fill is in a company that's rumored to be facing layoffs, and your candidates mention that they're reluctant to take a position in a company that's unstable. You may want to let them know that the job is in a department that's fiscally robust, so layoffs won't affect them.

Candidates give very common objections such as their tenure with the company.

The candidate that has been with the company for decades could be the perfect applicant

> **Beware!**
> The Do Not Call Registry is growing, so make sure that the people who are part of the list aren't on your calling list. These people don't want to get sales calls at their homes or businesses and by law, you have to comply. The web site is www.donotcall.gov.

because the client is looking for those same qualities. Or say your candidates would prefer higher pay. You may be able to assuage their concerns by letting them know about promotion opportunities at the client company. Whatever your selling point, make sure it's compelling and honest.

Rebuttals should also be honest responses and information or stories should never be fabricated to make a deal. You need to be steadfastly ethical when dealing with both candidates and clients. You don't want to build a business to have it crumble over something so trivial. If you cover up problems or inflate the truth, your candidate will likely find out and refuse any offer. Your reputation will also suffer. Reputation is everything in this business, so it's worth maintaining.

Screen Your Candidates

You've collected a list of candidates. During your interviews with them, how do you discern which ones are truly qualified and who you should present to the client? You don't want your skepticism to scare away a great candidate by sounding confrontational, but you also don't want to gloss over important questions and end up tarnishing your image.

- *Urgency.* If you presented an opportunity to them and facilitated a placement, would they be willing to submit their letter of resignation and start the new position within a month? If you offer to set up an interview and spell out a potential time frame and they balk, set that person in your tickler file or request a referral. You don't want to be stuck with a candidate that is "testing the waters."

- *Qualifications.* Are they a "fit" for the job? Does their past experience, skills, career goals and personality match the open position and client company culture? If they aren't the ideal candidate, don't force a "square" candidate into a "round" company/job. Keep them in your database in case you find a "square" job.

- *Motivation.* Are we seeing a trend? If you recognize the significance of the candidate's motivations and are intuitive enough to recognize them, you already have a major proficiency for this industry. For each candidate, ask their reasons for looking for a new position. If it isn't related to a layoff or a spouse's relocation, most people are seeking new opportunities that they aren't finding through their current jobs. Be wary of the "money only" response.

> ## Quick Quote
>
> Missouri entrepreneur Jeff H. says that "When you get the candidates and their resumes, you're only 40 percent of the way through the process."
> - Is the client a good fit?
> - Is the candidate a good fit?
> - Is it a good fit for the spouse, kids, and family?

These are only a few candidate qualifiers, but if you can figure out their "hot buttons" for making a change and what caused the candidate to shift from possibly annoyed with their employment situation to ready-to-take-my-plant-and-pictures-with-me-now mentality, you will have a good handle on your understanding of the candidate, which in turn gives you greater candidate control. You should have a solid understanding of the candidate before you put them in front of a client. Get used to aligning yourself with winning candidates and your clients will notice and make you a happy recruiter.

It's Not Just the Money

Candidates often express interest in a new job because they're looking for more pay. And recruiters often stress the salary as a selling point. But many times, especially with higher-level positions, candidates are looking for more than greenbacks.

People often seek out new challenges, including greater responsibility, a larger staff, leading a company in a different direction, expanding markets, or creating new divisions. Many also want to leave a highly structured corporation for a situation with more autonomy, where they can call the shots.

They may want to work for a more successful or exciting company, especially if their company appears to be on the skids. Or they may want to live somewhere that better suits their lifestyle, whether it is a big city, a small town, or suburbs with good schools.

Be sure to sniff out candidates' reasons for wanting to leave their current jobs. The more you know about why he or she is interested in a switch, the better job you'll do in selling the new position.

Get Those Glorious Referrals

Many new recruiters miss the value of the glorious referral. Finding ideal candidates by weaving your way through your referral list is a far better use of your time than cold-calling a pile of unrelated prospects. If you don't ask for a referral when you have someone captive on the phone, they will almost never volunteer them, so don't hang up without requesting one. Who cares if the person you are talking to isn't interested in the job? He knows someone who might be and that's a better phone call to make because you have the name of someone who told you to call and you already have an idea of their possible interest level. However, make sure that you have their approval to use their name.

Sometimes you will need to get creative when asking for referrals or candidate leads. Call the client's competitors and ask if they know of anyone who possesses the skills you need and it's possible they have resumes on file from previous searches. Who knows. You won't know if you don't ask.

Here are some recommendations for getting referrals:

- *Stay on good terms with fellow recruiters.* If you have a particularly difficult job order to fill, have a recruiter in your back pocket you can call that might be able

Job Specifications for a Project Director

○ *The client company.* Large, nonprofit health maintenance organization in the Midwest. Company employs 5,000 people, including administrators, practitioners, health-care educators, and others. The company is the leading health maintenance organization in the region, its market share is growing, and it is planning to expand outside the area.

○ *Location.* Dayton, Ohio

○ *Position.* The project director will manage a computerized health risk assessment and education tool for teenagers. This tool is provided by the HMO as a community service to schools and agencies. The director will implement the program in the community.

○ *Responsibilities.*

   • Supervising one staff member
   • Identifying sources of outside funding and preparing grant proposals
   • Representing the program to community and government leaders
   • Handling media and public relations

○ *Experience and background required.*

   • Five or more years project management experience in health care
   • Leadership and consulting skills
   • Excellent spoken and written communication skills
   • Ease in working with diverse populations
   • Must be willing to travel within region
   • Experience in writing grants
   • Experience in working with schools

○ *Education required.* An undergraduate degree, preferably in communications or public health.

○ *Compensation.* Between $56,000 and $84,000, plus retirement benefits.

Questionnaire for Project Director Position

Requirements	Yes	No
Five years' project management experience in health care	❏	❏
Experience in grant writing	❏	❏
Experience working with schools	❏	❏
Good communication skills	❏	❏
Willingness to travel	❏	❏
Bachelor's degree	❏	❏
Salary requirements	❏	❏

to point you to someone. Make sure that you are willing to return the favor when they are in the same position.

- *Keep up with the industry-specific directories.* Your trade specialty probably has one and you should know about it. If you don't, you know your next homework assignment.

- *Join networks.* You can join general networks or seek out niche networks to find new candidates.

- *Attend trade shows.* Each industry or specialty has at least one trade show a year and you need to go to them. If you're not, then you're already missing out on some face time with valuable candidates and market trend information.

- *Become an industry expert.* Nothing improves visibility than being involved in your community, chamber of commerce, local newspapers, writing articles for web sites or magazines, or conventions. Get out from behind your desk and get visible.

- *Get listed in the Kennedy Directory of Executive Recruiters published by Kennedy Publications.* The contact information is in the Appendix but most recruiters swear by this directory.

Protect
Yourself

Being an executive recruiter is occupationally risky because it is such an emotional people-based business. Candidates can change their minds, clients can pass on every candidate, or a current employer can decide that they can't do without the candidate and makes a counteroffer.

The Dreaded Counteroffer

Stat Fact

A recent poll by PowerHiring shows that if a candidate received two job offers with identical salaries, 36 percent said that the deciding factor would be corporate culture and quality of coworkers. 28 percent chose the company with professional development opportunities.

Few things are worse for a recruiter than losing an ideal candidate to a counteroffer made by their current employer. You made all three sales; you sold the client on their ability to find a candidate, sold the candidate on the idea of interviewing for the position, and then sold the client on the candidate. After all this recruiting "dating" happened and the client extends an offer to the candidate, the candidate gives an ultimatum to their current beau and the employer makes a counteroffer. All those hours and efforts lost, but even though it's a nightmare for the recruiter, they should have seen it coming.

It is the recruiter's job to make sure that the candidate is screened to see their true motivations for looking for another job. Are they just angling for a raise or promotion and want to get an offer that they can walk into their boss's office? That raise isn't going to pay you a penny. You are a professional, not a puppet.

Be honest with yourself with each candidate, and an ounce of skepticism never hurt anyone. Don't harp about counteroffers otherwise you may give the candidate the idea that maybe that's what they should do. Instead, ask them about their reasons for leaving. If they can't pinpoint one or it's just about salary or status, you might want to take a closer look at this candidate. Have they accepted a counteroffer before? If they have, it's more likely that they will do so again. Or if this is their first job change, they may be more inclined to accept since it's a perceived safer choice.

This is one "check" you want to make early on with each candidate in order to focus your efforts on candidates that are sincere about their move to another company. Other than saving yourself the hassle of losing a placement, you don't want the client to think you're sloppy about screening candidates.

So how do you forecast a counteroffer? There are a few common signs that should make you mark that deal as risky:

- *Have they put the hunt on hold?* If the candidate doesn't sound as enthusiastic for the search by throwing delays into the interviewing schedule, then that may be a warning sign. Candidates that don't make themselves readily available or avoid interviews by constantly rescheduling may be already changing their minds.

- *Can't make up their mind?* An evasive candidate who passively-aggressively delays making any decisions or constantly asks for more information probably wasn't ready to make a move yet or maybe wasn't even truly in the market.
- *Spreads the word?* A candidate that honestly wants to make a smooth transition doesn't trumpet the fact that he's got a better opportunity coming his way, especially if he hasn't been offered the position yet. Someone who tells coworkers or superiors about the potential job is angling for a counteroffer by applying pressure through gossip.
- *Requests an impromptu review?* Like the warning sign above, if the candidate is trumpeting his dissatisfaction about his compensation package and is holding your job offer as a threat to his supervisor, employers often call impromptu reviews to discuss a raise to keep them.
- *Didn't show you the resignation letter?* Always make sure you get to see a copy of their resignation letter because they may have slipped phrases in it that give the employer the impression that they are resigning against their will or were hoping that there could have been a growth opportunity that would have permitted them to stay. See the Sample Resignation Letter on page 126.

Most recruiters would prefer a bad cold-calling day over a lost candidate. It's your responsibility to always keep a keen eye out for the counteroffer risk, and if you don't trust that the candidate will follow through, move on to the next. Your time is valuable and you want to maintain a level of trust with the client.

Being a Matchmaker

Once you have a pile of resumes from candidates who are fairly close to fitting the requirements of the job, you need to start narrowing them down to get the best qualified.

The candidates may have answered "yes" to everything on your questionnaire, but you still don't know much about the specifics of their experience, personality, or work style. You may also have some questions about their resumes. Now's the time to conduct preliminary phone interviews to get a better feel for each candidate.

Say we're still looking to fill the HMO's project director job. We need someone who believes in the project (he or she will have to sell it to the community and organizations that grant funds), is comfortable working with teenagers, and has writing skills. The client company also mentioned that they're looking for someone with an outgoing personality, as the employee will be an advocate for the project. And you know from talking with people in the organization that this person will have to be fairly thick-skinned, as he or she will be working under a supervisor who lacks good interpersonal skills.

Sample Resignation Letter

Cathy Candidate
3214 Changing Way
Progress, RI 07686
(732) xxx-1234

August 30th, 20xx

Sandy Supervisor
Engineering Manager
Engineering Expert Enterprises
5332 Departing Lane
Progress, RI 07686

Dear Ms. Supervisor:

Please accept this letter as formal notification that I am leaving my position with Engineering Expert Enterprises on September 15. I will continue to support the projects assigned to me until that time.

I have enjoyed working under your supervision, and I appreciate the opportunity you have given me to apply my experience.

If I can be of any assistance during this transition, please let me know.

Sincerely,

Your Signature

Cathy Candidate

Set up a time to interview the candidate on the phone. You may have to set aside evening or weekend time, since your candidate may not be able to chat on the phone during the workday. When you get him or her on the phone, ask some general questions about his or her current job and the reasons he or she is interested in a new position. Be sure to get:

Smart Tip

Tip...

Use a friendly demeanor to help relax your candidates, but keep the conversation on track. You have a lot of phone interviews to make, so you can't waste too much time.

- A detailed description of his or her current responsibilities
- Major accomplishments on the job
- Current salary
- Reasons for interest in a new position
- Reporting relationships in his or her current organization

In our project director example, we also want to ask how the candidates feel about the project, whether they have any experience with teenagers (and whether it was good or bad), and what sort of writing experience they have. You may even ask for examples of past grant proposals written by the candidates.

Just by talking with a candidate, you'll get an idea of how outgoing he or she is. You should try to feel out the candidate's personality and work style: Will she fit into the rather formal environment of the HMO? What sort of hours can he keep? You should also get a feel for how interested the candidate is in the position. And you can tell how thick-skinned she is by asking questions about past difficulties with co-workers. If he seems to have had trouble with insensitive supervisors, that's a red flag. But if he seems to shrug off some incidents, that may be a good sign.

Getting to Meet the Candidates

After conducting preliminary interviews, you'll have narrowed the group down to five or ten candidates. These are the people who seem to have all the qualifications for the job. It's time to interview them in person, whether you meet them in your office or in a restaurant.

Beware!
In the United States, there are certain questions that are illegal to ask during an interview.

The recruiters interviewed for this book said they always try to interview candidates in person, but sometimes they have to conduct a second interview by phone. They'll do a phone interview if the position is not a very high-level one, if the candidate is far away, or if the client isn't willing to pay for candidates to travel for interviews.

You can meet the candidates in your office, at a restaurant, or in a rented room at an airport. Anyplace that's quiet and private will fit the bill.

Always be on time and dress professionally: you're projecting an image on behalf of the client, so you want to appear professional and competent. Remember, the candidates are assessing the company (represented by you) as much as you are assessing the candidates. If you're meeting in a restaurant, choose one that's fairly quiet and upscale—the kind of downtown restaurant that businesspeople in suits frequent. If you're renting a clubroom, rent one that has comfortable, well-kept furniture and offers some privacy.

For each interview, be sure to bring the candidate's resume and two lists of questions. The first list will be questions based on the position's requirements and what you know about the candidate so far. The second will be a list of general interview questions (see the List of Interview Questions on page 129). The candidate will likely have many questions for you, too, so be sure to also bring along as much information as you have (and are allowed to reveal) about the company and the position. Included in this chapter is a list of Questions the Candidate May Ask on page 131. You should be prepared to answer these items.

Spend a few minutes breaking the ice, but since you have a lot of ground to cover, don't chat for too long. Start asking questions in any order that feels right to you from college to the present, from the current job to expectations for a future position. Don't ask questions that the candidate can answer with a "yes" or a "no." Ask "why" and "what," and request specific examples. Take notes: you may be writing a report for the client later on.

In the interview process, you're trying to get a better picture of the candidate's personality, how well she communicates, what motivates her, her problem-solving skills, her interpersonal skills, her organizational ability, and any other areas your client wants covered. Go with your gut feeling—if something about a candidate seems off, pay attention to that feeling and ask questions until you feel you've uncovered the problem.

The interview should last between one and two hours. Immediately after the interview, write down your impressions. Depending on

> **Smart Tip** Tip...
>
> Try to let the candidate do most of the talking. If you're chatting away most of the time, you'll walk away with very little impression of the candidate. Shoot for spending three-quarters of the time listening, one-quarter talking.

the agreement you have with the client company, you may or may not send a written assessment of each candidate to the client. In either case, you'll want a written assessment of each candidate for your own records. Again, go with your intuition—if you get the impression that the candidate has a bad temper or is overly sensitive, write it down.

List of Interview Questions

These are some general questions to give you an idea of a candidate's motivation, as well as how he or she works with colleagues and approaches problems. You'll want to ask more questions that are specific to the industry and the position at hand.

1. With what sort of personalities do you work well? With what sort don't you work well? _____

2. What is the worst mistake you've made recently? _____

_____

3. What is the biggest challenge you've faced at work recently, and how did you resolve it? _____

4. What do you do if you feel your supervisor has made a mistake?

_____

5. How would your friends and family members describe your personality?

_____

6. What are your strengths and weaknesses? _____

_____

7. How do you motivate your subordinates? _____

_____

8. What projects at work have you taken on that you didn't have to do?

_____

9. What would you do differently in your career if you could start over?

_____

List of Interview Questions, continued

10. How do you handle the pressure of having too much to do?

   _____

11. Have you ever had a subordinate who wasn't performing, and if so, what did you do about it? _____

12. Describe your ideal supervisor. _____

   _____

13. What, if anything, would you do differently in your career? _____

   _____

14. How would you react if a subordinate told you that you'd made a wrong decision? _____

15. What sort of hours do you work? _____

   _____

16. What tasks do you delegate, and which tasks do you perform yourself?

   _____

17. What sort of challenges do you like? _____

   _____

18. What kinds of decisions are most difficult for you? _____

   _____

19. Do you ever take work home? _____

   _____

20. Why are you interested in leaving your current job? _____

   _____

Questions the Candidate May Ask

While the candidate will save most of his or her questions about the company for the client, you should also be prepared to answer some questions about the job and the organization. Below are some typical questions from job candidates.

1. How would you describe the culture at this organization? _____

_____

2. Who is the ideal employee for this position? _____

3. How do supervisors at this organization measure and review performance?

_____

4. What's a typical day at this job? _____

5. What do you think are the best and worst aspects of this job?

_____

6. What sort of hours do employees work? _____

_____

7. How do supervisors motivate their subordinates? _____

_____

8. How long do employees typically last in this position? _____

_____

9. What are the opportunities for advancement? _____

_____

10. Why did the previous employee leave this position? _____

_____

Questions the Candidate May Ask, continued

11. Please describe the organizational structure. _____

_____

12. Can you tell me who my manager would be? _____

_____

13. What sort of manager is this person? _____

_____

14. How many people would I be supervising? _____

_____

15. How does upper management view this department? _____

_____

16. What are the strengths and weaknesses of this department? _____

_____

17. What are the strengths and weaknesses of this company? _____

_____

18. What attributes are valued in an employee at this organization? _____

_____

19. What attributes are not valued? _____

_____

20. What is the history of this company? _____

_____

Value of Candidate Control

Recruiters refer to their struggle to understand and anticipate the behavior of their candidate as "control" and although it seems like a strong term, it can make or break a placement. They aren't saying that they manipulate or truly "control" a candidate; it refers to how well you may have selected the candidate, understood their true motivation for change, and if you have properly prepared the candidate to perform in front of the client. If you have a candidate that you don't know one day to the next how they might feel about a position or if they may change their mind entirely about making a move, then you can easily say that you have no control over this candidate.

Let's go back to the dating scenario. You have a friend and an acquaintance that you are setting up on a blind date. You have a good idea of how the friend is going to act ("client control") but you don't know what the acquaintance is really looking for or why they are single again (low "candidate control"), so you might not really know how the date will go and if they will ultimately hit it off. Either way, the result will be linked back to you because you made the match.

California entrepreneur Mark M. analogizes that "Recruiting is like a marriage. A bride that has debt or a groom who proposes more than once is like a candidate that accepts a job and then interviews for and takes another job. Good recruiters have control over jobs and candidates. You don't want any surprises at the altar."

Amateur recruiters miss the mark on the importance of control. Many of them don't focus much effort on each candidate and try the cooked spaghetti approach by just tossing a candidate against the wall to see if they stick.

There are numerous reasons why a candidate might be looking to make a move from their current employment situation and you may never know all the reasons but there are three that are common among most:

- *Personal.* Maybe it's a personal reason at work or home that is causing them to look elsewhere. For most, it's that they don't have solid relationships or they feel they are incompatible with others and it leaves them unfulfilled and disconnected. This could be tied to different goals, backgrounds, religions, educational experience, political views, or just that the corporate culture or aesthetics isn't a fit for them.

- *Professional.* For some, their career goals are stymied with their current employer or they don't feel that they can advance in their current position. As a recruiter, you want to focus on these reasons the most since you can't guarantee that they will like the employees any better at the next position. It's your job to focus on the professional needs of the candidate.

- *Situational.* Maybe it's neither of the above but they can't handle the commute or there are other outside factors that are influencing their reason to move.

Often family factors come into play and motivate the candidate to make a change.

It's important to know as much about the candidate's reasons as possible so that you can offer viable options. If you aren't aware of why they are leaving their employer, then they may back out entirely from the job hunt or play you as the pawn to extract a counteroffer. You have the jobs, so who should be in control?

13

Covering Your
Bases

Executive recruiting is a series of steps and it's important to cover your bases. Next, we will go over the background checks and the presentation of candidates to the client.

Sample reference and background check templates are provided in this chapter, to assist you with these important responsibilities.

The Background Checkup

Those of us who've made it past the age of, oh, say ten years old, have learned that people aren't always what they seem to be. You've got a candidate who looks great on paper, interviews well, and seems to have all the personality characteristics necessary for the position you're trying to fill. How do you know this person doesn't have a penchant for hitting on young interns, coming into work Monday mornings with an incapacitating hangover, or embezzling from employers?

Those are extreme examples (though employees have been known to do those things). More typically, a candidate inflates a resume to indicate that he or she earned a degree that was never granted, or held a higher-level position than is true. Either way, if you place someone with a closet skeleton, your reputation will be on the line.

Fun Fact

The most common embellishment on resumes, according to the recruiters interviewed for this book, is claiming degrees that were never granted.

Sample Applicant Information Release Form

I hereby authorize any person, educational institution, or company I have listed as a reference on my employment application to disclose in good faith any information they may have regarding my qualifications and fitness for employment. I will hold Placement Pals, any former employers, educational institutions, and any other persons giving references free of liability for the exchange of this information and any other reasonable and necessary information incident to the employment process.

Printed Name: _____

Signed: _____

Date: _____

Sample Personal Reference Check Letter

Placement Pals
345 Hiring Way
Job City, RI 55555

March 3, 20xx

Fiona Friend
9087 Friendship Way
Relationship, AL 44444

Re: Confidential Reference for Cathy Candidate

Dear Fiona Friend:

The above-named individual has applied for employment with our business and has named you as a reference. In order to make an informed hiring decision, we need to know the applicant's work/educational history and personal qualifications or fitness for employment. A release permitting you to provide the following information has been signed by the applicant and a copy is attached. Any information that you give will be held in the strictest confidence. Please verify by answering the following questions.

- How long have you known Cathy Candidate? _____
- What is the nature of your relationship? _____
- Why do you think Cathy Candidate would be a good choice for this position? ____

  _____

- Do you know of any reasons that could prevent Cathy Candidate from performing the functions of the position? _____

  _____

Information furnished by: _____
Signature: _____
Date: _____

Thank you for your cooperation and prompt response.

Sincerely,

Rena Recruiter
Placement Pals

Sample Educational Record Check Letter

Placement Pals
345 Hiring Way
Job City, RI 55555

March 3, 20XX

Universal Business School
Universal University
543 Education Way
Learning Lake, RI 55556

Re: Confidential Reference for Cathy Candidate
Graduate of Universal Business School

Dear Universal Business School:

The above-named individual has applied for employment with our business and has indicated that he/she obtained a degree from Universal Business School. In order to make an informed hiring decision, we need to explore the applicant's educational history and personal qualifications or fitness for employment. A release permitting you to provide the following information has been signed by the applicant, and a copy is attached. Any information that you give will be held in the strictest confidence. Please verify the information supplied by Ms. Cathy Candidate and answer a few questions regarding Universal University:

Degree received by Cathy Candidate: Bachelors of Science, Business Administration

Dates Cathy Candidate attended Universal Business School: 1980–1984

- Is the preceding information correct? _____
- Type and level of institution: _____
- Is your institution accredited? _____
- What types of degrees do you award? _____
- How can we obtain a transcript? _____
- Information furnished by: _____

Thank you for your cooperation and prompt response.

Sincerely,

Rena Recruiter
Placement Pals

Sample Employment Reference Check Letter

Placement Pals
345 Hiring Way
Job City, RI 55555

March 3, 20XX

Pete Personnel
Human Resources Manager
Gizmo Gadgets, Inc.
7890 Assembly Lane
Advancing, AL 44444

Re: Confidential Reference for Cathy Candidate
Filling Level 1 Engineer position, 199X–200X

Dear Mr. Personnel,

The above named individual has applied for employment with Placement Pals and has named you as a former employer. In order to make an informed hiring decision, we need to know the applicant's work history. Cathy Candidate has signed a release permitting you to provide us with the requested information, and a copy is attached. Any information that you give will be held in the strictest confidence.

Please verify employment by answering the following questions:

How long was Cathy Candidate employed with your company? _____

Please provide all dates of employment: _____

What position(s) were held by Cathy Candidate? _____

What was the Cathy Candidate final rate of salary?_____

How would you describe her work ethic and reliability? _____

_____

_____

Was Cathy Candidate's work satisfactory? (If no, explain) _____

_____

How did it rate to others in a similar position? _____

_____

_____

Sample Employment Reference Check Letter, continued

Please describe her strengths and weaknesses. _____

_____

_____

How were her written and verbal skills? _____

_____

_____

Were there any personal problems that affected her work? _____

_____

_____

Why did Cathy Candidate leave your company? _____

_____

_____

If an appropriate position were open with your company, would you rehire this person? _____

_____

_____

Additional comments: _____

_____

_____

_____

Information furnished by: _____

Thank you for your cooperation and prompt response.

Sincerely,

Rena Recruiter
Placement Pals

Sample Employment Reference Phone Script

Cathy Candidate has applied for a position with our business, Placement Pals, and you were listed as a former employer. Cathy Candidate has signed a release that authorizes you to give us the following information. [Give identifying information they ask for to help them find the applicant's file. You may have to offer to send a copy of the applicant's release to the former employer in order to get the information.]

Would you please verify that Cathy Candidate worked for your company from dates _____ to _____?

What was Cathy Candidate's job title? _____

Could you give me a brief description of the duties Cathy performed? _____

_____

Please verify that Cathy's final rate of pay was $ _____ hourly/weekly/biweekly/monthly/annually (circle one).

Was Cathy Candidate reliable? _____

Was the work Cathy performed satisfactory? _____

Did Cathy work well with coworkers and supervisors? [If applicable, with customers and/or clients?] _____

_____

What was the reason given for leaving your company? _____

_____

Would you rehire Cathy? _____

_____

Would you recommend Cathy Candidate for a position as a Level II Engineer? __

_____

Thanks for taking the time to speak with me. Is there anything else that you think I might find helpful in making a hiring decision with respect to Cathy Candidate?

_____

Beware!

If you have to leave a voice message when you're calling for a reference, don't give the name of the candidate. Just say you are calling to conduct a reference check. You never know who's going to listen to the message.

"The worst thing you can do as a search consultant is present a candidate who misrepresented something or had a hidden liability that you didn't find," says Ken C., our recruiter in Panama City Beach, Florida. "There's so much resume abuse, so much resume embellishment these days that you really better find out if someone's got an MBA from the University of Chicago before you accept the fact that they have one."

Some of the entrepreneurs we interviewed do more background checking than others. The amount of checking depends on whether the recruiter is retained or working on a contingency basis. Retained recruiters do more checking than contingency recruiters—clients understand that retained recruiters can afford to spend the time to check out background information because they're guaranteed payment for the job.

Ken C., who does retained searches exclusively, says that he always does a thorough background check. "One of the things I've accomplished in the interview is figuring out who are some people I know that I can talk to about [the candidate]." He then calls his acquaintances and asks if there's anything about the candidate that his client needs to know.

On the other hand, recruiters with a very focused specialty will know all the players, and background checks aren't so necessary. Donna K., who recruits market research candidates in the New York City area on a contingency basis, says, "It's a small industry. There are certain names that you know. Certain reputations will precede themselves. Having been in market research for eight years, I try very hard to interview my candidates and really get at their knowledge base rather than trying to nose around."

Higher-level positions also call for more background checking than lower-level ones. "We do background checks if something's off," says Tamara L., in San Mateo, California. "If it's a lower-level position and everything looks good, we don't worry about it. But on more senior people with certain clients, there's an expectation that we've asked around a little bit."

Finally, some clients will do their own background checks. Vivian K., who runs a search firm in Philadelphia, says many of her clients have a system in place for conducting background checks. "Because our search is on an

Beware!

In some states, it's illegal to record a phone conversation without consent of both parties. Check on this before you record any conversations. If you need consent, get it on tape.

Bright Idea

If you don't have any mutual acquaintances with your candidate, call his or her previous employer. This person should be able to give a good portrait of your candidate.

hourly basis, background checking is a service they can opt for. We ask them if they want us to check references or not."

Candidates always supply names of people who can give them references, but you need to do more than call these people. References are usually friends of the candidate who aren't going to give the whole truth. Call the references, but also check that the candidate really did earn the degrees listed on the resume.

A really thorough background check also includes a check of criminal records, credit history, and a search to see if the candidate has been mentioned in the media. You don't have to do all this yourself—look in the Yellow Pages under "Investigators" to find a service that does this kind of work.

Finally, you want to call anyone you know who also knows the candidate. It's much better to call someone you know for a reference, as a friend or acquaintance is going to be much more candid than someone you've cold called. Even if you're calling the

Extensive Background Check Components

Here is a list of the background checks many recruiting companies complete on candidates prior to placement.

- ○ Employment and earnings history
- ○ Workers' compensation history (by state)
- ○ Previous employment confirmation
- ○ Educational and professional license verification
- ○ Personal reference check
- ○ Criminal conviction history (by state)
- ○ National wants and warrants
- ○ Civil records
- ○ Federal records
- ○ Bankruptcy records
- ○ Credit report
- ○ Driving record
- ○ Drug testing

friend of a friend, you're still better off. If someone referred you to the candidate, he or she is also a good source.

Ask your references if there's anything you should know about the candidate and double-check information such as why the candidate left a job, what the duties were, whether he or she would be welcome back in the organization. Listen very carefully—for tone, pause, and hesitation.

Many people are afraid of giving bad references. "You need to ask the right kind of questions," says Manny A., the Chicago entrepreneur. "You need to just keep listening to what they're saying. You're not listening to what they're saying as much as how they're saying it and what they're not saying." As you did with interviews, you'll want to write up a report of what the references you consulted said about each of your candidates.

Tread Carefully

Making background checks is risky business, so you must be very careful how you do it. "When you do back-door references, you run the risk of their boss finding out that they're looking, and that's not particularly cool," warns Donna K.

Don't let your sources know that the candidate is actively searching or is under consideration for a position. You can say that you haven't spoken to the candidate yet, but you've heard good things about this person and you were wondering what your source thought before you give the candidate a call. It's also a good idea to ask your sources not to mention that you were calling for a reference. When your candidate is unemployed and openly seeking, you can be a little more relaxed.

If you come across any skeletons through reference checks, ask the candidate about it. He or she may have a good explanation that you can verify. Or, your candidate may deny it despite some evidence to the contrary. If that happens, try to find out as much information as possible, and listen to your gut instinct about who's telling the truth and who's not. You may just have to make a judgment call. Just as you can't take a candidate at face value, sometimes you can't take a reference at face value, either.

So you shouldn't discredit a candidate because you hear some negative remarks. Just be sure to let your client know, preferably in writing, if you come across anything in the background checks. This will help cover you legally in case the candidate is hired and something goes wrong.

However, if you find something in a candidate's background that you believe could create serious problems for your client, you should not refer that candidate to the client. Tamara L. adds that while one bad reference may not mean anything, "I do know that if you talk to four or five people, and they all say he was a mistake to hire, then that means something."

Sample Reference Check Form

Applicant Name: _____

Position: _____

Personal references checked:

Name: _____

Relationship: _____

Address: _____

Telephone: _____ Date contacted: _____

Method of contact: _____

Notes: _____

_____

- -

Name: _____

Relationship: _____

Address: _____

Telephone: _____ Date contacted: _____

Method of contact: _____

Notes: _____

_____

_____

- -

Name: _____

Relationship: _____

Address: _____

Telephone: _____ Date contacted: _____

Method of contact: _____

Notes: _____

_____

Sample Reference Check Form, continued

Employment references checked:

Name: _____

Employer: _____

Relationship: _____

Dates of employment: _____ Pay: _____

Address: _____

Telephone: _____ Date contacted: _____

Method of contact: _____

Would you rehire?: _____

Reason for termination: _____

Notes: _____

_____

- -

Name: _____

Employer: _____

Relationship: _____

Dates of employment: _____ Pay: _____

Address: _____

Telephone: _____ Date contacted: _____

Method of contact: _____

Would you rehire?: _____

Reason for termination: _____

Notes: _____

_____

- -

Name: _____

Employer: _____

Relationship: _____

Sample Reference Check Form, continued

Dates of employment: _____ Pay: _____

Address: _____

Telephone: _____ Date contacted: _____

Method of contact: _____

Would you rehire?: _____

Reason for termination: _____

Notes: _____

_____

- -

Name: _____

Employer: _____

Relationship: _____

Dates of employment: _____ Pay: _____

Address: _____

Telephone: _____ Date contacted: _____

Method of contact: _____

Would you rehire?: _____

Reason for termination: _____

Notes: _____

_____

- -

Records checked:

School records (date requested: _____)

Notes: _____

Criminal records (date requested: _____)

Notes: _____

Driving records (date requested: _____)

Notes: _____

Credit records (date requested: _____)

Notes: _____

Smart Tip *Tip...*

Check out Entrepreneur.com/ FormNet for free download-able forms, samples, checklists, and worksheets.

It's not only unethical to refer a candidate when you know there's a problem, it's professionally damaging—your success depends on the success of your candidate. If you place a problem candidate, your reputation will be on the line.

Importance of Interview Prep

So you have what you think is the ideal candidate for the job order. Now you have to send them in to interview with the client without you. You won't be there to coach them or make sure that they didn't spill coffee on themselves on the way over, and you can only hope that they showcase all of the reasons why you feel they are a great candidate in the first place.

The entrepreneurs interviewed for this book said that they will sometimes prepare their candidates and their clients for the interview. But they're cautious about creating an entirely new image for the candidate—after all, they need to act in the best interests of the client, rather than the candidate. However, they sometimes find a candidate who they believe is highly qualified and who would make an excellent fit, but needs some help polishing their interview skills.

In that case, they'll do a small amount of interview preparation. "You have to let that individual fly on their own," says Manny A. "You might do a little more coaching on how they might present themselves, but not to the extent that you make a different person out of them."

Unfortunately, people can act differently with a recruiter than they do with the client, so to avoid any interview disasters (and they do happen—check out some horror stories from our experts from the web sites listed in the Appendix), you might need to gently prepare your candidate for the interview.

1. *Walk through the interview.* Talk to your candidate and discuss their responses to various questions that could be asked. Make sure to go over their strengths that they want to showcase. Don't have them leave the interview without covering the basics. It's fine if they talked about their mutual love of golf, but the fundamental info needs to be exchanged too. You're not getting paid to find someone a golf buddy.

Smart Tip *Tip...*

Want more info on this topic? Check out Bill Radin's articles: "Seven Keys to Interview Success" and "How to Master the Art of Interviewing" at www .billradin.com.

2. *Give them confidence.* A candidate that has been adequately briefed will feel more confident about the interview and do better than one sent in blindly. Make sure you go over any concerns that they may have so that they don't get caught off-balance with a question they weren't prepared to answer.

3. *Encourage them to be enthusiastic.* Remind the candidate that the client wants someone who likes doing their job and that they should convey that interest. Be enthusiastic but not ecstatic. Even if the candidate is usually a reserved person, remind them that this is the time to come out of their shell.

4. *Plan your time.* By practicing with you, the candidate can better utilize the time allotted for the interview and allow enough time to focus on their successes. This also makes the role for the client easier since the candidate will have an idea of what they would like to cover, which often makes the interview go smoother instead of putting that responsibility solidly on the client.

5. *Keep it short and sweet.* When an interviewer asks a question the candidate can either give the long answer or the short and sweet answer. Help you candidate craft the short and sweet versions of their stories and remind them to tell the interviewer that there is a longer version if they would like to know more.

6. *Give them an idea of the "soft" fit.* There are many intangibles that the client is looking for in a candidate to see if they will fit in well with the company that the candidate should be aware of such as the corporate culture or personality. If you properly inform your candidate of these traits that go beyond their basic qualifications, there is a better chance for chemistry or "fit" between the client and candidate. You wouldn't want something as simple as miscommunication about the company culture to disqualify an ideal candidate.

Vivian K. adds that she also shies away from too much coaching. But she will try to make things go more smoothly, if necessary. For example, she once had a candidate who was interviewing with two managers, both of whom spoke English as a second language. She warned the candidate about this: "I told him to eliminate all slang."

The Presentation

Now that you've checked up on your candidates, you should be ready to present the finalists to the client. Retained recruiters say they aim for two to five finalists—clients want to be able to choose, but they don't want to be overwhelmed. The recruiters present them all at once, and then the client interviews the candidates and makes a choice.

Contingency recruiters tend not to limit the number; instead, they refer qualified candidates as soon as they find them. Because they're often in competition with other

Presenting . . .

Manny A., who runs a recruiting firm outside Chicago, says clients will often ask him which of the three or four candidates he's presenting to them is the best. He's learned that doing so is a big mistake. "You never, never rank them in order of who you think is the best," he says. If you do, the client will ask to see the best one. And if the client doesn't like that person, he or she won't want to see No. 2 and No. 3.

All the candidates you're presenting are qualified for the position, Manny advises, so the person who's the "best" is entirely up to the client. You may think one person is the best, but the client may have an entirely different point of view. It comes down to chemistry between the candidate and the client. "The client might see [a problem] you didn't," he says. On the other hand, "Someone else you think is [just] OK, they'll think is the greatest thing since sliced bread."

recruiters or the client's human resources department, they want to move as quickly as possible.

When you're ready to present your candidates, give your client a detailed description of each one—personality, experience, education, including weaknesses and strengths. Also, forward the resumes and summaries of initial interviews and reference checks.

Also, if a recruiter has a candidate who's eminently qualified but doesn't interview well, he or she may tell the client that. "I might say, 'Look, this guy is a little quirky,'" says Vivian. "'But he's just going to be at a desk by himself.'"

The Match

Once you've presented your candidates to your clients, it's time to sit on the sidelines and let the client make a choice. Our recruiters say this is often the most difficult part of the search process because it's out of their hands.

If the matchmaking hits a snag, such as a candidate who wants more money or a client that didn't like any of the candidates presented, the recruiters we interviewed say they jump in and help with negotiations. They may try to convince the candidate that the money is the best he or she can do, or they may try to talk the client into accepting someone who has a little less experience than the job description required. But they try not to make too hard a sell.

Smart Tip

As soon as the client has selected a finalist and the candidate has accepted, inform all the other candidates who are waiting to hear. As a courtesy, let them know—diplomatically—why they weren't chosen. If it was a matter of chemistry, tell them their qualifications were excellent, but the clients felt another candidate fit their company's culture better.

Donna K. says she tends to hang back a little if she can see why the candidate doesn't want to take the job. "If I have an offer out to a candidate, and they're not thrilled with the offer, and they're not thrilled with the company, I find it very hard to sell it. You let them make their own decision." She adds that this attitude helps her in the long run, because it builds trust with that candidate.

Jeff H. says that "You need to coach them in. There are lots of feelings and emotion with making a job change. There are many analogies to dating and marriage with executive recruiting."

Keeping in
Shape

Agood deal of a recruiter's job has little to do with searching for and placing candidates. There's lots of back-burner work that recruiters need to do to keep their businesses humming. They need to continually expand their network if they want to fill jobs. They also need to maintain good client relations by presenting quality candidates and maintaining their integrity throughout the search process. Finally, they must keep up on the news about their specialty. In this chapter, we'll look at some of the ways recruiters can keep their businesses in good shape.

Ease of Movement

The recruiters we interviewed say that the recruiting process doesn't stop when a candidate accepts a job offer. Recruiters should continue courting the candidate right up to the first day of work. They frequently find that they'll get involved in details such as salary and benefit negotiations, job descriptions or relocation details. Sometimes they even help the new employee get along with supervisors or co-workers.

Mark M. says that, "You're only at the ten yard line at a football game when the client is placed." Staying in touch with the client and candidate after the placement is important to make sure that it is a fit.

Many times both the client and the candidate will turn to the recruiter with questions about the other party. Candidates and clients often ask recruiters questions they didn't feel comfortable asking each other, such as expected work hours and possible personality conflicts.

As our recruiter Donna K. notes, because she's an outsider, it's often easier for her to talk with the candidate and the client than it is for them to talk with each other. "It's a very psychological position," she says. "I spend most of my time being a therapist."

And if the client and candidate reach an impasse over salary or benefits, the recruiter often tries to work it out. The recruiter may explain to the client that a candidate of a certain caliber demands a higher salary, or explain to the candidate that the client simply can't offer more but may be able to in the future.

Also, recruiters sometimes help a candidate transition into the job. They'll help a candidate move, find a home, even research schools. They may also step in once the job starts to help ease any conflicts. "We hook people up with people who provide relocation services," Tamara L. says. "I've booked flights for people and taken their wives out to dinner—that kind of thing."

The recruiters we interviewed say they try to make the job move as easy as possible on everyone because then everyone will view it as a success. "A seamless transition has a lot more possibility of sticking," says Tamara.

Bright Idea

Once an offer is made and accepted, make sure your client and your candidate put it all down on paper. That way the salary, benefits, and expectations are clear, and if there's a conflict down the road, at least there's a memo that states what the intentions were.

Personal Notes

Besides just being a good, trustworthy recruiter, it also helps to personally connect with the client a little. We all want to work with people who like us and take an interest in our lives. When you're talking with your clients, you'll naturally hear some details about their personal lives—their children's school, their new home, their boyfriend's name. Make notes in your database or your address book (wherever you can easily access them when you're on the phone) and ask about these things next time you talk.

You can say, "How's your daughter's new school working out?" Or, "Have you settled into the house yet?" Or, "Did Gary [the boyfriend] ever sell his car?" The client will be flattered that you remembered and cared to ask. And it makes it easier for them to call you for a job the next time. Just be sure to limit the chitchat to no more than a few minutes. You do want to appear professional and efficient, after all.

Donna K. says that she'll stay in touch with the candidate until the job starts. Then she makes a check-in call about a month later to see if everything's going smoothly. "It there's a problem, I'll try to get involved and do some counseling," she says. "Sometimes it's just a matter of communication."

Our recruiters note, however, that taking part in these negotiations can be tricky. While they want everyone to be happy with the match, they need to keep in mind that they're serving the client—after all, that's who pays the checks. And a client who is happy with a good placement is more likely to seek the recruiter's assistance again.

Manny A. stresses that recruiters should always remember that they're acting on the client's behalf. Donna K. adds that she tends to back off if she feels that the match isn't quite right. "I'm not a hard-core salesperson," she says. "If you have to bow out gracefully, you bow out gracefully."

It's Who You Know

The more people you know in your specialty, the better recruiter you'll be. You'll have more potential clients, more names to call to find candidates, and more people who can give you background information on candidates. Even when you're not trying to find people to fill a specific position, it's always good to build your database for future jobs.

Tip...

Smart Tip

Carry a notebook or electronic organizer with you at all times, even when you're not officially working. You never know where you might run into someone who'd make a good addition to your database.

So how do you build your database? You network. Tamara L., who runs a firm in San Mateo, California, says she always makes an effort to attend social and business events. She chats with other guests, asks what they do, tells them her line of business, and hands out business cards. She puts everyone she meets in her database—just about anyone who could help her out in her work someday.

Donna K., whose business is in New York City, adds that she'll take note of any names she comes across, whether in the media, from conversations with people in the business, or at conferences. She'll add a name to her database even if she hasn't met the person.

"I'll hear a name in my networking, in my travels, and maybe their title is appropriate," she says. "I'll just call and introduce myself."

Larry D. in Huntersville, North Carolina, joined associations for his specialty—human resources personnel. Some of them give out a directory of their members, and they hold meetings where he can network with people in his field.

Happy Client, Happy Recruiter

Of course, maintaining a huge database of potential candidates is only part of the equation. You must also know how to keep your clients happy, because if there are no clients, there are no job orders to fill—and there is no paycheck.

First, always conduct yourself in a professional, courteous, and friendly manner toward your clients. "Part of it is having a good personal relationship," says Larry D. "They know if they call me, I'll call them back."

Naturally, doing a good job—finding candidates your clients want to hire—goes a long way toward developing a good relationship. And in the process of selecting and presenting candidates, you must maintain your integrity: Send only quality candidates, and always be honest with your clients.

"You're in it for the long haul, and maintaining a relationship with a client is very, very important," insists Manny A., our executive recruiter in Chicago. "That client is the best source for another assignment. That client is going to remember you as someone who helped them out when they needed it. One of the things you learn very early in the game is that you have to conduct yourself in a very ethical manner."

Bright Idea

Do a newsgroup search online to find people in your specialty. You may find a few bulletin boards or newsgroups where potential contacts hang out.

It may be tempting, especially for contingency recruiters, to send just about any candidate to the client, hoping that one of them will fit the bill. But that's not the way to win clients. They're hiring you to select and screen candidates so they don't have to spend the time doing it. The client wants to interview just a handful of highly qualified candidates and make a selection from that group. "My clients know if I say somebody's good I mean it," Larry D. says.

"My clients know me as someone who sends four or five resumes for a position and every person is appropriate," says Donna K. "I'm not the type of recruiter who just sends resumes out there with the theory that if you throw enough at the wall something's going to stick. I personally don't believe in doing that, and I've made my reputation as a recruiter who doesn't do that. If I really strive to find the right person for the position, someone who's going to stay, everyone's happy, and they'll refer me to someone else that they know."

It also may be tempting to inflate a candidate's qualifications so the client will hire the candidate and you'll get the commission. But this will only backfire on you. If the candidate doesn't work out, you may have to return your commission, and you'll likely lose a client—especially if they realize you weren't upfront about the candidate's background.

"From what I see in the retained world, there's a tendency to oversell the candidate or to bypass possible negatives," says Vivian K., who operates a retained search firm in Philadelphia. "We try to think of ourselves as an extension of the human resources function. So we're really evaluating the candidates."

Vivian adds that if she's having trouble finding candidates who fit the qualifications, she'll let the client know rather than try to mold candidates to make them fit the position. For example, a client might want some highly experienced candidates but is unwilling to pay the salary such experience demands. Vivian says she'll give them an honest assessment of the situation: "I might say 'At this compensation, these are the best people out there. They might not interact as professionally with the senior team as you might want. I can present to you two more people who are beyond the compensation range who I think are what you want. And you can make a decision on that basis.' By being trustworthy," she adds, "you earn their trust."

Smart Tip

Tip...

You should present at least two, and no more than five, candidates for each position. Your clients want to make a choice, but they don't want to interview more than a handful of candidates.

News of the Specialty

You want to know the characters in your field, but it also helps to know what's happening in a larger sense. To stay competitive, you'll need to know if an employer is laying off workers, planning to hire a whole new cadre of employees, or opening or closing a certain line of business.

If a business is laying off workers, you'll know that employees there will be ready to jump ship, so that business will make a good source company. If a business is hiring, give them a call and pitch your services. You'll also want to know where the job growth is. Perhaps your particular specialty is getting phased out in many businesses, but there's a related field that's growing. You might want to redirect your area of specialty.

So how do you get this information? Read, read, read—and listen. Follow all the media about your business: the mainstream press, the business pages of local and national newspapers, trade journals, and web sites. Also attend any association functions. At these mixers you'll hear what's happening before the press does and you'll be ahead of the game. "We do a lot of reading," says Tamara L. "Every weekend is just catching up on what the trends are."

To track emerging trends that can affect small businesses in general and your recruiting industry, you need to stay informed. Use the Trend Analysis Worksheet on page 159 from Entrepreneur.com to help you stay on top.

Trend Analysis Worksheet

❑ Read a major metropolitan newspaper regularly, as well as one or two papers serving your local community. This way, you can stay informed on current events on both local and global scales.

❑ Join associations that serve your industry. To find an appropriate association, consult the *Encyclopedia of Associations*, published by Gale Research. You can find this publication in larger libraries.

❑ Keep track of bestselling nonfiction books. Although these books may not always apply directly to your business, they may reveal trends that you can use to your advantage.

❑ Contact government agencies or consult government publications for industry-specific information. The departments of Commerce and Labor as well as the Census Bureau, for instance, have data tracking various industry trends. You might also consult large libraries (particularly those in large public universities) for information gathered by the government. Such libraries often have sections devoted to government publications.

❑ If you have access to an online information service, you might be able to find a source of the latest information on your industry.

❑ Subscribe to relevant trade periodicals and newsletters. Many trade associations publish periodicals, which are usually filled with valuable management tips, industry trends, etc.

❑ Attend industry conventions and seminars. These venues offer an exciting array of information regarding specific industries as well as new training methods.

❑ Read journals and magazines on a local as well as national level that deal with small-business or business in general. Publications like the *Wall Street Journal* and *Entrepreneur* are valuable sources of trends that are developing on a national scale, and of detailed information on specific business opportunities. Local business journals that cover key developments in your own community are also important because you can track new ideas and trends that appeal to a specific geographic market.

Find more forms for your business at www.entrepreneur.com/formnet.

15

All About
Employees

Though the majority of the executive recruiting business start-ups are one-person operations, you may want a larger company. The best case would be if you started your business and you saw the opportunity to expand. Whatever the case, it's a good idea for you to understand the human resources aspect of owning a business.

In this chapter, we'll talk about the hired help: personal assistants and other recruiters, as well as contractors you can hire to help you with your searches. We'll look at ways to find employees for your firm and how to train, compensate, and motivate them. We'll also delve into the contractors you can use to help speed your searches: search researchers, who find candidate names for you, and investigators, who can check out candidate backgrounds.

Assistant Aid

There's no need to hire an employee for your recruiting business. A good phone system, a well-organized database, and any word processing program will perform secretarial duties admirably. And if you don't hire anyone, you won't have to worry about all the legal requirements involved in setting hours, writing paychecks, granting leave, and so on.

That being said, all the entrepreneurs interviewed for this book have assistants—someone who answers the phone, schedules interviews, books flights, and orders office supplies. They perform basic secretarial duties. Sometimes these employees also research companies and potential candidates. The recruiters we interviewed say that they found their time too valuable to spend performing these administrative tasks.

Being recruiters, our entrepreneurs had no trouble finding their assistants. They tended to acquire them through networking and contacts. And, of course, recruiters know how to interview and assess skills.

The Recruiting Crew

Hiring another recruiter to help you with your business is a double-edged sword. There are some great advantages, but also some real drawbacks. First, we'll deal with the plusses: It can bring more money into your business. Since you typically take a percentage of an additional recruiter's income, you'll earn some of what they earn without doing the recruiting work.

Having one or more recruiters working for you also helps you draw clients. You'll always have the bodies available to do the work that comes your way, so clients will know that they can call you and get someone on a job quickly. Some of the recruiters we interviewed hired additional recruiters to work for them when they found they had too much work on their

> **Quick Quote**
> Entrepreneur Jeff H. warns that about "Nine out of ten recruiters don't make it within the first two years."

hands. "It just kind of happened," says Vivian K., who runs her firm in Philadelphia. "I got so booked in the beginning that I hired someone just to help me with the overflow."

But hiring recruiters has some serious drawbacks. Once you hire a recruiter, you'll need to train and manage him or her in ways that you don't need to do with an assistant. The work they do is much more involved and far more delicate—especially if they're interacting with clients—so you'll need to oversee them closely.

Two of our recruiters had additional recruiters work for them in the past, but no longer. Manny A. in Chicago says that he simply grew tired of managing. At one point he had 12 people working for him; now it's just his assistant and himself. Ken C., who recruits out of Panama City Beach, Florida, says he's much happier without a crew. "I make more money and have a whole lot more freedom and control of my life when I can do the work myself and not spend my time babysitting," he says.

So, while you take a cut of an additional recruiter's pay, you may end up working for that money in the time you spend managing the employee. Tamara L., who has a firm in San Mateo, California, says that she spends most of her time managing her 11-person office and very little time recruiting. While she says she finds some of the managing rewarding, she misses recruiting. And she's no longer bringing in the income she once was.

You may find that you enjoy managing, that you're successful at training recruiters, and that it benefits you financially. Or you may find you hate having to answer questions and resolve problems that aren't your own, and you're much better at just recruiting. It depends mostly on your skills and personality—and whom you find to work for you. A resourceful, independent recruiter is going to take less of your time than someone who likes reassurance every step of the way. And an experienced one is going to ask far fewer questions than one who has never recruited before.

Staffing Up

How you organize your firm will have as much to do with your own preferences as it will with your employees' skills. If you have someone who's great at working online but shy about making phone calls, you may have yourself a great researcher. On the other hand, if your employee has a knack for bringing in clients, you'll want to take advantage of that skill.

Most of the recruiters interviewed for this book said that they hired people as they came along. It wasn't part of their plan to hire recruiters, but they found someone they felt would be successful and would work well in their business.

Larry D. in Huntersville, North Carolina, said that he found his two recruiters through his web site. "If I see that they're local and their background looks good, I hire them," he says. He didn't set out to hire employees, "I just hired them if it seemed like they were going to work out. I'm always open to hiring people as I identify them or find them."

Donna K., in New York City, hired someone who came through her office as a candidate. The employee had never recruited before, but she was interested in the work and had the right personality for the job. And because she was in the market research field—Donna's specialty—she had contacts in the industry and knowledge of its practices. Tamara L. hired people she and her partners knew through their contacts.

Stat Fact

The average turnover in brick-and-mortar executive search firms nationwide is around 80 percent. That means that if you are like most other firms, if you hire 10 new recruiters at the beginning of the year, you will probably have only 2 at the end of the year. Don't be offended if they don't stick around for long.

It's Your Property

Databases, date books, and address books—including names, phone numbers, job titles, email addresses, and client lists—are the property of the recruiting company, not the recruiter. So if an employee leaves your company, these items need to stay with you.

If you have an employee you suspect or know is planning to leave for another recruiting firm, you should be extremely vigilant in making sure the database stays inside your company. You may need to remind your employee that the database is the property of the company, and taking it constitutes stealing.

If you fire an employee, or if someone leaves under bad circumstances, make sure you don't give the employee the chance to steal the database. Watch over these employees as they clean out their desks, and escort them to the door.

The recruiters we interviewed considered their hires carefully but warn that it's impossible to know for sure whether someone is going to work out. Recruiting is a real sink-or-swim kind of business, and sometimes the only way you'll know if someone will be successful is to throw him or her into the pool.

Tamara L. hired one recruiter who was a "great schmoozer, great with clients," she says. "I thought he'd be fantastic. I probably spent two hours a day for almost six months trying to get him to be successful." She finally had to let him go—he just didn't have the attention to detail needed to be a successful recruiter. And Donna K.'s recruiter left after eight months—while she was successful finding and interviewing candidates, she didn't feel comfortable with the selling side of the job.

The recruiters we interviewed who employ additional recruiters use them in a variety of ways. Some let the employees find their own clients and job orders, and conduct their own searches. Other recruiters had their employees act as assistants who conduct the name search and the initial screening, but don't handle the final interviews or interactions with the clients.

The advantage of letting your employees find their own clients and job orders is that you do less managing; the advantage of having them do the locating and screening work only is that you can save your time for managing the all-important client relations. Vivian K., who has her employees conduct the initial work, says that she wanted to save her clients the irritation of hearing from too many people at her firm. "I wanted to maintain that relationship," she says.

Protect Yourself

If you're worried that your employees might leave after a short time and start their own businesses, taking some of your clients with them, you might want to consider having them sign a noncompete clause. Check with an attorney about this—a noncompete may or may not be enforceable, depending on where your business is located.

When you are bringing an employee on board, it's important to protect yourself since you are opening your business to them. Two sample non-compete agreements are provided on pages 166 and 167, to tailor to your needs to ensure that the information from your office isn't being shared, nor can your employee use the experience with you to become a direct competitor.

> **Bright Idea**
> Don't pay a departing employee his or her commission until the guarantee periods have expired. If a placement leaves before the time is up, you'll have to refund the money, and it'll be a tough fight getting that money out of an ex-employee.

Sample Non-Compete Agreements

Example 1

This example is a complete agreement that you can fill in and use for an employee who does not have a separate written employment contract.

Non-Disclosure and Non-Competition. (a) At all times while this agreement is in force and after its expiration or termination, [employee name] agrees to refrain from disclosing [company name]'s client lists, trade secrets, or other confidential material. [Employee name] agrees to take reasonable security measures to prevent accidental disclosure and industrial espionage.

(b) While this agreement is in force, the employee agrees to use [his/her] best efforts to [describe job] and to abide by the nondisclosure and non-competition terms of this agreement; the employer agrees to compensate the employee as follows: [describe compensation]. After expiration or termination of this agreement, [employee name] agrees not to compete with [company name] for a period of [number] years within a [number] mile radius of [company name and location]. This prohibition will not apply if this agreement is terminated because [company] violated the terms of this agreement.

Competition means owning or working for a business of the following type: [specify type of business employee may not engage in]

(c) [Employee name] agrees to pay liquidated damages in the amount of $[dollar amount] for any violation of the covenant not to compete contained in subparagraph (b) of this paragraph.

IN WITNESS WHEREOF, [company name] and [employee name] have signed this agreement.

_____
       [company name]

_____
       [employee's name]

Date: _____

Sample Non-Compete Agreements

Example 2

This example is part of a larger agreement, such as an employment contract or an employee handbook. You can use it as a separate agreement or incorporate it into another, larger document.

Non-Disclosure and Non-Competition. (a) After expiration or termination of this agreement, [employee name] agrees to respect the confidentiality of [company name] patents, trademarks, and trade secrets, and not to disclose them to anyone.

(b) [Employee name] agrees not to make use of research done in the course of work done for [company name] while employed by a competitor of [company name]

(c) [Employee name] agrees not to set up in business as a direct competitor of [company name] within a radius of [number] miles of [company name and location] for a period of [number and measure of time (e.g., "four months" or "10 years")] following the expiration or termination of this agreement.

(d) [Employee name] agrees to pay liquidated damages of $[dollar amount] if any violation of this paragraph is proved or admitted.

IN WITNESS WHEREOF, [company name] and [employee name] have signed this agreement.

_____
[company name]

_____
[employee's name]

Date: _____

Staff Training

Many small businesses conduct their "training" just by throwing someone into the job, but that's not fair to the employee, and it's certainly not good for your business. If you think you can't afford to spend time on training, think again—can you afford not to adequately train your employees?

In an ideal world, employees could be hired already knowing everything they need to know. But this isn't an ideal world, and if you want the job done right, you have to teach your people how to do it.

Chances are good you're not going to find a recruiter with tons of experience to work for your firm. After all, when experienced recruiters can start up their own businesses, why would they work for someone who'll take a cut of their pay?

Most everyone interviewed for this book says that they hired people with no recruiting experience: "Our whole mentality was that we'll bring on anyone who's smart and sharp, and has an idea of what the work is," says Tamara L., "then we'll give them a lot of detail about the work and teach them about recruiting."

Whether done in a formal classroom setting or on the job, effective training begins with a clear goal and a plan for reaching it. Training falls into one of three categories: orientation, which includes explaining company policies and procedures; job skills, which focus on how to do specific tasks; and ongoing development, which enhances basic job skills and grooms employees for future challenges and opportunities. These tips will help you maximize your training efforts:

> **Tip...**
>
> **Smart Tip**
> Training employees—even part-time, temporary help—in your way of doing things is important. They represent your company and need to know how to maintain the image and standards you've worked hard to establish.

- *Find out how people learn best.* Delivering training is not a one-size-fits-all proposition. People absorb and process information differently, and your training method needs to be compatible with their individual preferences. Some people can read a manual, others prefer a verbal explanation, and still others need to see a demonstration.

- *Be a strong role model.* Don't expect more from your employees than you are willing to do. You're a good role model when you do things the way they should be done all the time. Don't take shortcuts you don't want your employees to take or behave in any way you don't want them to behave. On the other hand, don't assume that simply doing things the right way is enough to teach others how to do things. Role-modeling is not a substitute for training; it reinforces training. If you only role-model but never train, employees aren't likely to get the message.

- *Look for training opportunities.* Once you get beyond basic orientation and job skills training, you need to constantly be on the lookout for opportunities to enhance the skill and performance levels of your people.

- *Make it real.* Whenever possible, use real-life situations to train—but avoid letting clients know they've become a training experience for employees.

- *Anticipate questions.* Don't assume that employees know what to ask. In a new situation, people often don't understand enough to formulate questions. Anticipate their questions and answer them in advance.

- *Ask for feedback.* Finally, encourage your employees to let you know how you are doing as a trainer. Just as you evaluate their performance, convince them that it's OK to tell you the truth, ask your employees what they thought of the training and your techniques, and use that information to improve your own training skills.

So chances are good that you'll have to show your new hires the ins and outs of recruiting. Manny A. says he drew up a notebook describing the process of finding and placing candidates. "The notebook had the things you do that make you successful in this business," he says. "But it wasn't a bible they had to follow. I attempted to help them understand the methodology, introduced them to clients, [and] helped them draw in new clients."

Tamara L. gives new recruiters an orientation program that outlines the recruiting process. Then the partners of her business develop a script the new recruiters can use when they place their calls to candidates. For the screening interviews, she says, "There's a checklist you want to go through: why are you looking to leave your current position, what do you want to do next, how soon do you want to make a move?" The scripts ensure that new recruiters cover all the bases in approaching or screening candidates.

Vivian K. uses a mentoring approach in training her new employees. "We're very hands-on with them in the beginning in terms of writing scripts for what they're going to say—how they'll capitalize on the best aspects of the position," she says. "They put a script together, then they e-mail it to me, and we talk about it. And then they make refinements. There's a script for voicemail, and there's a script for live. For those first ten calls, you always need a script."

Larry D., who purchased a franchise, said that he receives help from his franchisor in

> **Smart Tip** Tip...
>
> Start your new recruiters out on your lowest-level positions with your less important clients. That way, if they make a mistake, there will be less to lose.

training employees. The franchisor has an extensive training system in place that it applies to franchise employees.

The Motivation

Recruiters who work for other recruiters typically work on a commission basis. They receive a percentage—about 50 percent—of the fee they receive when one of their candidates is hired. If recruiters bring in the clients, they often receive more—in the range of 65 percent. And after they've been working for a while, they frequently receive a higher percentage.

Because they can't work without being paid, legally and practically, recruiters often receive a draw against future commissions when they first start out. So they'll receive a paycheck for the first few months, and as they start to bring in money, their employers subtract the money they've already received from their commissions.

Those employees who work on only part of the recruiting process, such as researchers and workers, who do initial screenings, frequently receive a salary, between $25,000 and $75,000 a year. Vivian K. pays all her employees a salary, though she gives bonuses based on the company's performance. Manny A. paid his employees a minimal salary plus a commission.

Money, of course, is the biggest motivator, but there are other ways to keep your employees happy. Recognition for a job well done always helps keep your employees—whether they're recruiters, researchers, or administrative assistants—performing up to par.

If someone has done a good job, always tell him or her. It's surprising how far a few words will go. But giving bonuses based on good performance helps even more. Tamara L.'s company puts its money where its mouth is: "Every time someone places a person, we walk around to everyone gets and give them $50," she says.

Employee Benefits

The actual wages you pay may be only part of your employees' total compensation. While many very small companies do not offer a formal benefits program, more and more business owners have recognized that benefits—particularly in the area of insurance—are extremely important when it comes to attracting and

> ## Smart Tip
>
> Tip...
>
> Draw up a contract, preferably with the help of a lawyer, between you and your employed recruiter regarding your commission policy. This will avoid major headaches, and possibly lawsuits, down the road.

retaining quality employees. In most parts of the country, the employment rate is higher than it's been in decades, which means competition for good people is stiff.

The law requires employers to provide employees with certain benefits that are not optional:

- Give employees time off to vote, serve on a jury, and perform military service.
- Comply with all workers' compensation requirements.
- Withhold FICA taxes from employees' paychecks and pay your portion of FICA taxes, providing employees with retirement and disability benefits.
- Pay state and federal unemployment taxes.
- Contribute to state short-term disability programs where they exist.
- Comply with the Federal Family and Medical Leave Act.

Typical benefits packages include group insurance (your employees may pay all or a portion of their premiums), paid holidays, and vacations. Some services offer year-end bonuses based on the company's profitability. You can build employee loyalty by seeking additional benefits that may be somewhat unusual—and they don't have to cost much.

Some other employee perks could be low or no-cost ideas like these:

- *Work from home days.* If you have your employees work from a commercial office, set them up to work at home a few days a week.
- *Community service days.* Give your employees a few paid days each year to take part in community or charitable activities that they may not have time for otherwise.
- *Pizza Fridays.* Bring pizza or sandwiches into the office every Friday. It doesn't matter what you bring but make sure to treat to whole office. A couple of pizzas might only cost you $20 or so.
- *Movie tickets.* Another $20 idea is to offer a pair of movie passes to an employee each month. This may be a way of rewarding a star employee or just as a morale booster.
- *Free car washes.* A basic car wash costs about $5 so offer a free car wash to your employees every once in a while. It's not the money you put in but the thought and the reward of giving them a shiny clean car to use for the rest of the week.
- *Continental breakfasts.* It may not be a free lunch but a free breakfast every once in a while always brightens a morning. Think of alternating it with other perks so it doesn't become an expectation and fixed cost.
- *Holiday parties.* You may not have a big office or a large staff, but celebrate the holidays and throw a party anyway. Celebrate with your staff and their families and see the morale boost through the New Year.

▲

Hang Back

Y ou can teach your recruiters your own method of finding and placing candidates, but you can't expect them to behave exactly as you would. Every recruiter needs to use his or her own strengths in matching candidates with clients.

Some people are geniuses at the soft sell; others do better when they come on strong. And a search firm with people of varying and complementary talents will be a stronger one for it. Your approach to selling a position may fail with a certain type of candidate, yet one of your recruiters may know exactly the right words to use. Or one recruiter may be brilliant at coming up with ways of finding candidates, and another may be a genius at placating the clients.

So teach your recruiters the basics, and then let them use their own creativity and experience in searching and matching. Try to hang back and give advice only when it's entirely necessary or requested. If your employees see that you trust them and expect them to perform well, they'll likely rise to the occasion.

Workers' Compensation

If you have any employees, even just one part-time employee, you are required in all 50 states to purchase workers' compensation insurance. This coverage pays medical expenses and replaces a portion of the employee's wages if he or she is injured on the job. Although the chances of such an injury are low in this industry, even if you have only one or two employees, you may want to consider this coverage to protect both them and you in the event of an accident, or if they develop any physical problems related to repetitive motion, such as carpal tunnel syndrome from typing.

The rate depends partly on your track record, so once you've been operating for a while, you may be able to get a lower rate. Executive search firms can expect to pay between 2 and 5 percent of their annual payroll. For example, if you pay $100,000 a year in salaries, you'll pay between $2,000 and $5,000 a year in workers' compensation

> **Tip...**
>
> ## Smart Tip
> No matter how much you enjoy your work, you need an occasional break from it, whether it's to take a vacation or to deal with an illness or personal emergency. Be sure your employees are well-trained and committed to maintaining your service levels whether you are there or not.

Bright Idea

If you have employees, consider using a payroll service rather than trying to handle this task yourself. The service will calculate taxes; handle reporting and paying local, state, and federal payroll taxes; make deductions for savings, insurance premiums, loan payments, etc.; and may offer other benefits to you and your employees.

insurance. Details and requirements vary by state; contact your state's insurance office or your own insurance agent for information so you can be sure to be in compliance.

Contracting Out

If you need help but you don't want the headache of managing a staff, there's an easy way out. You can always contract out for a researcher—someone who'll help you find names, screen candidates, and perform background checks. Large search firms employ researchers, but if you're a solo or small operation, you probably can't afford to pay someone full time. Fortunately, many researchers work as freelancers.

Ken C., the recruiter in Panama City Beach, Florida, uses freelance researchers extensively. In fact, he's compiled a directory of freelance researchers (see the Appendix) with the tasks they perform and the rate they charge.

Ken strongly recommends that recruiters hire researchers who charge by the hour rather than by the name. "The people who charge by name aren't so good," he says. "The people who bill like that are not legitimate research assistants. There's no way to predict how long it's going to take to generate one name or 50 names, so the legitimate researchers won't guarantee one price. If you do that, either you're making up names, or you don't have a good handle on your own costs." Freelance researchers charge about $100 an hour.

Freelance researchers, because they work outside your organization, will have a different approach to finding candidate names. You may find you're always heading down the same path, trying to beat the same names out of the same bushes. A contractor could hand you a set of resumes you'd never find yourself. If you want to conduct a credit or criminal check, you can hire a freelance researcher, or you can hire an investigator (try the Yellow Pages under "Investigators").

It's also important to be sure your independent contractors meet the requirements set by the IRS. A sample independent contractor agreement from SmartBiz.com that they designed to help draft a custom agreement that fits your needs are provided on page 174.

Beware!

Always try to get a referral for a contractor before you hire one. You don't want to waste valuable time on someone who can't produce names. If you can't get a referral, try out a researcher or investigator on a smaller or less time-sensitive project first.

Independent Contractor Agreement

This Agreement is entered into as of the [   ] day of [   ], 20[   ], between [company name] ("the Company") and [service provider's name] ("the Contractor").

Independent Contractor. Subject to the terms and conditions of this Agreement, the Company hereby engages the Contractor as an independent contractor to perform the services set forth herein, and the Contractor hereby accepts such engagement.

Duties, Term, and Compensation. The Contractor's duties, term of engagement, compensation and provisions for payment thereof shall be as set forth in the estimate previously provided to the Company by the Contractor and which is attached as Exhibit A, which may be amended in writing from time to time, or supplemented with subsequent estimates for services to be rendered by the Contractor and agreed to by the Company, and which collectively are hereby incorporated by reference.

Expenses. During the term of this Agreement, the Contractor shall bill and the Company shall reimburse [him or her] for all reasonable and approved out-of-pocket expenses which are incurred in connection with the performance of the duties hereunder. Notwithstanding the foregoing, expenses for the time spend by Consultant in traveling to and from Company facilities shall not be reimbursable.

Written Reports. The Company may request that project plans, progress reports and a final results report be provided by Consultant on a monthly basis. A final results report shall be due at the conclusion of the project and shall be submitted to the Company in a confidential written report at such time. The results report shall be in such form and setting forth such information and data as is reasonably requested by the Company.

Inventions. Any and all inventions, discoveries, developments and innovations conceived by the Contractor during this engagement relative to the duties under this Agreement shall be the exclusive property of the Company; and the Contractor hereby assigns all right, title, and interest in the same to the Company. Any and all inventions, discoveries, developments and innovations conceived by the Contractor prior to the term of this Agreement and utilized by [him or her] in rendering duties to the Company are hereby licensed to the Company for use in its operations and for an infinite duration. This license is non-exclusive, and may be assigned without the Contractor's prior written approval by the Company to a wholly-owned subsidiary of the Company.

Confidentiality. The Contractor acknowledges that during the engagement [he or she] will have access to and become acquainted with various trade secrets, inventions, innovations, processes, information, records and specifications owned or licensed by the Company and/or used by the Company in connection with the operation of its

Independent Contractor Agreement, continued

business including, without limitation, the Company's business and product processes, methods, customer lists, accounts and procedures. The Contractor agrees that [he or she] will not disclose any of the aforesaid, directly or indirectly, or use any of them in any manner, either during the term of this Agreement or at any time thereafter, except as required in the course of this engagement with the Company. All files, records, documents, blueprints, specifications, information, letters, notes, media lists, original artwork/creative, notebooks, and similar items relating to the business of the Company, whether prepared by the Contractor or otherwise coming into [his or her] possession, shall remain the exclusive property of the Company. The Contractor shall not retain any copies of the foregoing without the Company's prior written permission. Upon the expiration or earlier termination of this Agreement, or whenever requested by the Company, the Contractor shall immediately deliver to the Company all such files, records, documents, specifications, information, and other items in [his or her] possession or under [his or her] control. The Contractor further agrees that [he or she] will not disclose [his or her] retention as an independent contractor or the terms of this Agreement to any person without the prior written consent of the Company and shall at all times preserve the confidential nature of [his or her] relationship to the Company and of the services hereunder.

Conflicts of Interest; Non-hire Provision. The Contractor represents that [he or she] is free to enter into this Agreement, and that this engagement does not violate the terms of any agreement between the Contractor and any third party. Further, the Contractor, in rendering [his or her] duties shall not utilize any invention, discovery, development, improvement, innovation, or trade secret in which [he or she] does not have a proprietary interest. During the term of this agreement, the Contractor shall devote as much of [his or her] productive time, energy and abilities to the performance of [his or her] duties hereunder as is necessary to perform the required duties in a timely and productive manner. The Contractor is expressly free to perform services for other parties while performing services for the Company. For a period of six months following any termination, the Contractor shall not, directly or indirectly hire, solicit, or encourage to leave the Company's employment, any employee, consultant, or contractor of the Company or hire any such employee, consultant, or contractor who has left the Company's employment or contractual engagement within one year of such employment or engagement.

Right to Injunction. The parties hereto acknowledge that the services to be rendered by the Contractor under this Agreement and the rights and privileges granted to the Company under the Agreement are of a special, unique, unusual, and extraordinary character which gives them a peculiar value, the loss of which cannot be reasonably or adequately compensated by damages in any action at law, and the breach by the

Independent Contractor Agreement, continued

Contractor of any of the provisions of this Agreement will cause the Company irreparable injury and damage. The Contractor expressly agrees that the Company shall be entitled to injunctive and other equitable relief in the event of, or to prevent, a breach of any provision of this Agreement by the Contractor. Resort to such equitable relief, however, shall not be construed to be a waiver of any other rights or remedies that the Company may have for damages or otherwise. The various rights and remedies of the Company under this Agreement or otherwise shall be construed to be cumulative, and no one of the them shall be exclusive of any other or of any right or remedy allowed by law.

Merger. This Agreement shall not be terminated by the merger or consolidation of the Company into or with any other entity.

Termination. The Company may terminate this Agreement at any time by 10 working days' written notice to the Contractor. In addition, if the Contractor is convicted of any crime or offense, fails or refuses to comply with the written policies or reasonable directive of the Company, is guilty of serious misconduct in connection with performance hereunder, or materially breaches provisions of this Agreement, the Company at any time may terminate the engagement of the Contractor immediately and without prior written notice to the Contractor.

Independent Contractor. This Agreement shall not render the Contractor an employee, partner, agent of, or joint venturer with the Company for any purpose. The Contractor is and will remain an independent contractor in [his or her] relationship to the Company. The Company shall not be responsible for withholding taxes with respect to the Contractor's compensation hereunder. The Contractor shall have no claim against the Company hereunder or otherwise for vacation pay, sick leave, retirement benefits, social security, worker's compensation, health or disability benefits, unemployment insurance benefits, or employee benefits of any kind.

Insurance. The Contractor will carry liability insurance (including malpractice insurance, if warranted) relative to any service that [he or she] performs for the Company.

Successors and Assigns. All of the provisions of this Agreement shall be binding upon and inure to the benefit of the parties hereto and their respective heirs, if any, successors, and assigns.

Choice of Law. The laws of the state of [ ] shall govern the validity of this Agreement, the construction of its terms and the interpretation of the rights and duties of the parties hereto.

Arbitration. Any controversies arising out of the terms of this Agreement or its interpretation shall be settled in [ ] in accordance with the rules of the American

Arbitration Association, and the judgment upon award may be entered in any court having jurisdiction thereof.

Headings. Section headings are not to be considered a part of this Agreement and are not intended to be a full and accurate description of the contents hereof.

Waiver. Waiver by one party hereto of breach of any provision of this Agreement by the other shall not operate or be construed as a continuing waiver.

Assignment. The Contractor shall not assign any of [his or her] rights under this Agreement, or delegate the performance of any of [his or her] duties hereunder, without the prior written consent of the Company.

Notices. Any and all notices, demands, or other communications required or desired to be given hereunder by any party shall be in writing and shall be validly given or made to another party if personally served, or if deposited in the United States mail, certified or registered, postage prepaid, return receipt requested. If such notice or demand is served personally, notice shall be deemed constructively made at the time of such personal service. If such notice, demand or other communication is given by mail, such notice shall be conclusively deemed given five days after deposit thereof in the United States mail addressed to the party to whom such notice, demand or other communication is to be given as follows:

If to the Contractor: [name]
                                             [street address]
                                             [city, state, zip]

If to the Company: [name]
                                             [street address]
                                             [city, state, zip]

Any party hereto may change its address for purposes of this paragraph by written notice given in the manner provided above.

Modification or Amendment. No amendment, change or modification of this Agreement shall be valid unless in writing signed by the parties hereto.

Entire Understanding. This document and any exhibit attached constitute the entire understanding and agreement of the parties, and any and all prior agreements, understandings, and representations are hereby terminated and canceled in their entirety and are of no further force and effect.

Independent Contractor Agreement, continued

Unenforceability of Provisions. If any provision of this Agreement, or any portion thereof, is held to be invalid and unenforceable, then the remainder of this Agreement shall nevertheless remain in full force and effect.

IN WITNESS WHEREOF the undersigned have executed this Agreement as of the day and year first written above. The parties hereto agree that facsimile signatures shall be as effective as if originals.

[company name]   [contractor's name]

By:_____   By:_____

   Its: [title or position]   Its: [title or position]

SCHEDULE A

DUTIES, TERM, AND COMPENSATION

DUTIES: The Contractor will [describe here the work or service to be performed]. [He or she] will report directly to [name] and to any other party designated by [name] in connection with the performance of the duties under this Agreement and shall fulfill any other duties reasonably requested by the Company and agreed to by the Contractor.

TERM: This engagement shall commence upon execution of this Agreement and shall continue in full force and effect through [date] or earlier upon completion of the Contractor's duties under this Agreement. The Agreement may only be extended thereafter by mutual agreement, unless terminated earlier by operation of and in accordance with this Agreement.

COMPENSATION: (Choose A or B)

A. As full compensation for the services rendered pursuant to this Agreement, the Company shall pay the Contractor at the hourly rate of [dollar amount] per hour, with total payment not to exceed [dollar amount] without prior written approval by an authorized representative of the Company. Such compensation shall be payable within 30 days of receipt of Contractor's monthly invoice for services rendered supported by reasonable documentation.

B. As full compensation for the services rendered pursuant to this Agreement, the Company shall pay the Contractor the sum of [dollar amount], to be paid [time and conditions of payment.]

16

Advertising and Marketing

Even the most experienced recruiters find that they still need to drum up new business. In this chapter, we'll give you some tips on how to keep the work coming in, including obtaining job orders from previous clients, finding new clients, and riding out a slump in your industry.

Drumming Up New Business

All the recruiters interviewed for this book emphasize that they have to continually drum up work—they can never let business development slide, even if they're swamped with work. If you do, you'll have no new job orders to fill once your current candidates are settled in their jobs.

"You always have to spend part of your time developing business," says Larry D., the recruiter in Huntersville, North Carolina. "Otherwise, when you get finished, you might be looking at a blank piece of paper with nothing to do. You have to try to work a balanced day, with part of the day focused on marketing, part on recruiting."

Larry says he tries to market while he recruits: When he makes a call to a potential candidate, he pitches his services as a recruiter. It works well for him, since he specializes in placing human resources personnel—just the people who are likely to hire him to find candidates.

Now one big mistake is that some recruiters try to distinguish themselves from the next recruiter based on service. Well, if you are honest and adhere to the industry code of ethics, how much different could you really be than the next recruiter? One thing for sure is you don't want to be that 5th recruiter that finds the same resume on a job board and e-mails it to the client crossing your fingers that you actually get paid for it.

Instead, focus on benefits. There is more to this job than trying to be the first or fifth one to send in the same resume off the internet. Instead, here are a few ways to focus your efforts to showcase your benefits:

- *Specialize, specialize, specialize.* You will need to choose a specialty and become a master of that niche, but by knowing where to find the best talent, you offer your expertise as a benefit. You will save the client time by presenting a qualified candidate and they will respect your professionalism and resourcefulness. Once you're tagged as an expert, you are likely to have an edge on the next order.

- *Be perceptive.* A resume is such a minimal explanation of a candidate's capabilities, so you need to be able to perceive their other assets and be intuitive enough to recognize any shortcomings. A good recruiter is savvy enough to properly screen a candidate and judge whether they are right for the client or be honest and admit that there may be problems down the road. The client will appreciate your good judgment and consideration. Unfortunately, recruiters that are just out there to get rich quick will just throw candidates at the clients and hope that one sticks. Recruiting is shouldn't be like cooking spaghetti.

- *Earn their loyalty.* If you were a hiring manager, you would prefer to work with only three recruiters instead of thirty, right? When you add more recruiters, they can overlap and become difficult to manage. If you are professional, efficient and honest, you can build a relationship where you become one of their chosen few. Clients also want to align themselves with a recruiter that they think will stay in the industry, so even if you are a newbie, you need to prove that you're in for the long haul.

- *Show your dedication.* Here's another case why the active recruiters reign supreme over the passive online surfing ones. If you are willing to do whatever it takes to get the right candidate, it shows. Cold-calling is one of the main reasons why you are making money, because those easy-to-find candidates could have been found with their own staff. Show that you are willing to make the calls necessary to find the candidate for them.

Jeff H. says that when a client is considering hiring a recruiter, they are assessing their "reputation and probably more important is their 'access' to the top talent. Just because a recruiter has been in the business a long time or says they know a lot of people, doesn't give them 'access' to talent. Just because they can get someone on the telephone doesn't mean that candidates will trust them enough to share their career. This takes a recruiter who people respect and trust with their confidential information."

Ken C., who works out of Panama City Beach, Florida, says he puts aside one day a week to drum up new business. "I generally use Fridays to run through my Rolodex and my files, and think about who I can call and where I can find more business," he says. "You must reserve 10 to 20 percent of your time for business development, even when you're really busy."

He's been working in the business so long he no longer needs to do cold calls, but he still needs to keep in touch with clients. He dials their numbers and chats with them on the phone. He talks about sports, events—what have you—he says. Every so often, he adds, he'll send out a mailer reminding his clients of his successes in recruiting.

Manny A., who works outside Chicago, says that he remains active in a number of clubs to keep up his business contacts. It works, he says, because, "Invariably the conversation goes to 'What do you do?'"

Tamara L., in San Mateo, California, says she uses her network of friends and social contacts to help spread the word about her firm. She talks about her work, asks what people do, and passes out her cards. "You really have to get out there," she says, "to John's birthday party or Susan's wedding—all that sort of stuff."

Approaching It Cold

As we mentioned earlier, you'll be making lots of cold calls when you first start your business. As time goes on, you'll likely make fewer of these, but until you've been in the business for 20-plus years, you can count on having to pick up the phone to dial someone you don't know.

We talked about making a list of potential client companies. You should keep expanding this list as you come across names of people in companies in your field, or as you hear of new businesses or new divisions of old businesses. As you read trade journals or the business pages, note all the people who could be clients—anyone who has the authority to hire, including human resources personnel and managers—and record them in your database.

Every year or so, take a new trip to the library and research your potential client companies. You'll find a host of new possible clients each time you go. Keep a running list of names to cold call. Try to contact different people within the same company.

Beware!

Many prospective clients are going to be very nice to you even when they never intend to hire you. They figure that you'll stay away from their employees when you're searching for other clients if they give the hint that they may become a client someday. Any company that treats you well but never gives you work can be considered a source company (a source of candidates).

Once you have a list, set aside some time—a few hours each day or one day a week, whatever suits you—and make those calls. It may help you to write up a script including your specialty, your experience, and the fact that you're available to fill a position.

If you get voicemail, either leave a message and call back after a week if there's no return call, or hang up and call again until you reach a live voice. Once you've spoken with someone, keep track of the response. If it's an unequivocal "no," make a note in your database to call a year later. By that time, there may be someone new in that position, or circumstances may have changed enough to turn the "no" into a "yes."

If it's a "maybe," note in your database to call once a month or so until you either get a "yes" or a "no." And if it's a "yes," you've got work to do!

Donna K. in New York City says that cold calling is always "hit or miss." She says, "Sometimes I call, and they'll ask for references or names of other clients. Or I might have to really build the relationship and continue to call once a month until they have a position. Other times I'll call and say 'Hello, this is my company, and I specialize in market research. I heard through the grapevine that you may have an opening,' and they'll go 'Yeah, what's your fee?' So you really never know."

Keep building your database of potential clients and keep on top of the calls you need to make. By doing so, you'll continue to build your client base.

Other Ways to Sell Yourself

While many businesses benefit from well-placed advertisements, recruiting isn't one of them. Recruiters generally don't pay for advertising, and none of the recruiters interviewed for this book said they had even tried it. "It's really ineffective," says Paul Hawkinson of *The Fordyce Letter*. "Recruiting is a smile-and-dial business." He adds that paying for a regular space in a trade journal may help clients remember a recruiter's name, but cautions that, "Not very many clients are going to pick up the phone based on an ad."

Hawkinson suggests instead that recruiters can promote themselves by making speeches at clubs or writing articles for trade journals. Recruiters can always give expertise on finding or interviewing candidates, and they can also act as experts in their specialties.

If you want to write an article, call the editor of a trade journal and pitch your ideas. These might include a how-to article on finding good candidates, interviewing prospective employees, or negotiating a salary package. They could also be news articles on trends in the business, such as a shift in educational requirements or a new attitude about part-time work.

You can cover these same topics in a speech, as well. Local social and business clubs, such as the Rotary Club or the chamber of commerce, are often looking for speakers at their regular meetings.

In a Slump

It happens to all recruiters, even those specializing in the hottest of markets. Invariably, the economy, or the sector of the economy their specialty is in, goes south.

What do you do? You may find that you have to spend a greater amount of time developing business. But before you call everyone hoping for a lead, you should plan your strategy.

One way to go is to alter your specialty to a market that's more lucrative. It may not make sense to switch fields completely, but you may find a related field that offers more business.

Tamara L. says that when she saw the management consulting business start to flounder, she moved into wireless and internet infrastructure. "If that's where the money is, that's where we'll go," she says.

Another tack is to burrow into your specialty to find the positions that are hardest to fill. Even if the chemical engineering industry has hit an all-time low, there are likely to be some positions that are still hard to fill. Perhaps chemical engineers with experience in certain

> **Bright Idea**
> When you're expanding your client base, look at the companies closest to you geographically. Sometimes clients are more comfortable working with recruiters in their neck of the woods. When you've exhausted that list, expand the circle wider.

substances are still a hot item. Keep asking your clients what positions they have the most trouble filling, and you'll have an idea of where you should focus your attention.

A slow market calls for more than fine-tuning your specialty. You should also take a good look at your clients. If your clients are instituting hiring freezes or even laying off workers, they're not likely to ask for your services. In fact, these companies make great source companies, as many employees will be looking to jump ship.

Seek out those companies that are doing well despite the slump, and you'll be much better off. Ken C. says the key to staying afloat in a recession is choosing the right company: "You have so few clients that picking your client is a lot more important than the state of the economy. One person's market share is so miniscule that the economy could be doing great and you could have no business. Or the economy could be in lousy shape, but if you pick a growing company, you could be as busy as could be."

17

Paying
the Bills

Now that we've covered the basics of running a recruiting business—finding clients, searching and placing candidates, and marketing—we'll get down to the nitty-gritty of financial management. This chapter will focus on your monthly income and expenses, setting your fees, and paying taxes—all the things you need to think about to make sure you stay in the black.

When Money Comes Your Way

One downside of the recruiting business is that you can't count on even a minimal monthly income. You may make 12 placements a year, but those checks aren't going to arrive neatly on the first of every month. You may have no income for two or three months, then get a pile of checks all in one day.

If you've been working in the business for a while, you may have an idea of how much you can earn in a year. If not, keep in mind that the average annual gross pay for this business is about $100,000 a year, which works out to $8,333 a month.

Remember that you won't get any commissions for a few months at least, so you'll need to make sure that you can cover your expenses—business and personal—until the checks start arriving. Our experts and recruiters recommend that you have enough cash to cover you for six months. Once you start receiving the commissions, you'll need to budget carefully, because you can't count on a steady paycheck. So, before you really open shop, it's a good idea to work out your monthly expenses.

The Expense of the Business

To consider monthly expenses, let's go back to the example of Rena Recruiter, who's trying to decide whether to start with a homebased business or open a five-person office.

If she starts small, with a homebased business and no employees, the exercise will be simplicity itself. Rena can count on paying a phone bill and an internet service provider fee. The phone charges will total about $600 a month, including service charges, local and long-distance calls, and voicemail. The internet service provider will run her about $20 a month and Web hosting will cost $10 a month. She should add about $20 a month for miscellaneous office supplies (pens, paper, and sticky notes), and count on about $15 per month for legal fees. Her business insurance should be part of her homeowner's or renter's insurance.

So she's looking at $665 a month in business expenses, for a minimal homebased operation.

Bright Idea

Photocopy checks before depositing them. That way, if a collection problem occurs later, you have the client's current bank information in your files—that makes collecting on a judgment much easier.

Stat Fact

It's common knowledge in the industry that if you have a recruiting team, that there is an 80/20 rule. Like most sales offices, 80 percent of your revenue comes from 20 percent of your recruiters.

Of course, if she wants to use her home phone and already has a connection to the internet, as well as voicemail, she'll need to pay only for the higher monthly phone bill.

On the other hand, Rena might want to run a bigger firm with three recruiters and an administrative assistant. Naturally, she'll need an office for all these people. Let's say she finds a nice 1,500-square-foot retail space at $1.50 a square foot, for a monthly rent of $2,250. It has enough room for each person to have a private office, plus a conference room for interviews. Rena figures paying for the conference room space will save her money in the long run, as she and her recruiters won't have to spend time traveling to cafes and restaurants.

Each person will need an internet connection for an approximate total of $250 a month. Since the administrative assistant won't be making nearly as many calls as

Hiring Mathematics

You may think that you can earn lots of dough just by hiring a pile of recruiters to work for you. After all, recruiters earn about $100,000 a year, and you can take 50 percent of their salaries.

But it's not that simple. If you look at the Monthly Income and Expenses chart on page 193, you'll notice that Rena Recruiter's five-person office will bring in less than her home office will. If she goes the office route, she'll have overhead costs: rent, insurance, workers' compensation, and higher accountant's fees.

Consider, also, that Rena has to manage employees and the office. She's spending valuable time mentoring, supervising, and conducting managerial tasks such as signing paychecks and hiring employees. Not only are these tasks a burden; she'll earn a lower salary because of it.

That's why two of our recruiters, Ken C. in Panama City Beach, Florida, and Manny A. in Chicago, once ran offices with several recruiters but are now solo operations. Of course, if you run a virtual office, like Vivian K. in Philadelphia, you can cut out the expense of renting office space. Vivian's employees all work out of their homes. So think twice before you start hiring recruiters, or you could lose in the long run.

the recruiters, Rena can count on a total monthly phone bill of $2,500, including voice-mail, basic service, and local and long-distance calls. Insurance for the office totals $600 a year, so the monthly expense equals $50. Workers' compensation also has to be factored into the insurance costs, at 2 to 5 percent of the monthly payroll, or $525.

Finally, there are the salaries. Rena can expect to pay an administrative assistant about $30,000 a year, or $2,500 a month. And the recruiters, who should pull in salaries equal to Rena's, will be earning 50 percent commission, so Rena will have to pay them each $50,000 a year, or a total of $12,500 a month.

You'll also want to offer benefits to these employees because they're not likely to take the job without them. You can expect these benefits to cost about 30 percent of their paychecks, so you're looking at an additional $4,500 a month. A Sample Start-Up Expenses Sheet is provided on page 194.

Setting Fees

As we mentioned, most recruiters charge a percentage of the annual salary earned by the candidates they place. The fee is generally between 20 and 35 percent, and it applies to the salary the candidate and the client negotiate, not the salary posted. Say you succeed in filling a position that's listed with a $90,000 annual salary, and you charge a 25 percent fee. If the candidate manages to get the company to agree to $100,000 a year, you'll actually receive $25,000. This is true for both contingency and retained recruiters.

All the recruiters interviewed for this book, save one, charge a percentage of the annual salary. Some of them, the more experienced ones, have fixed rates that they won't change for any client, but the others say they'll lower their fees if necessary. Donna K., in New York City, says she charges between 20 and 30 percent, depending on the client and the job. "It's what they'll agree to," she says.

Some recruiters also take a percentage of the perquisites their candidates receive, such as hiring bonuses or the value of a company car or benefits. And some charge for expenses, such as travel and phone calls. The people who are able to command these fees tend to have a lot of experience. Ken C. in Panama City Beach, Florida, and Manny A. in Chicago, both of whom have

Bright Idea

Call your competitors—the recruiters who make placements in your area of specialty—to see what they charge. You don't want to go too low, as clients will think you're cutting corners. And you don't want to go too high, as clients won't pay you more to do the same thing another firm will do for less. Start your fees somewhere in the middle. A recruiting mentor can also help you decide your fee structure.

been in the business for more than 20 years, charge for expenses. Ken also figures the perks into his 30 percent commission.

Tamara L., the recruiter in San Mateo, California, gives a discount to customers who give her several assignments. Her firm charges 30 percent of the salary, but if a client wants five searches, the fee drops to 27.5 percent, then to 25 percent if the client needs ten searches. It's easier for her firm to conduct a number of searches for one client than a number of searches for several different clients, so that justifies the lower price. And dropping the price for volume work encourages clients to stick with her firm.

Jeff H. advises clients against requesting reduced fees. "Many companies will try to negotiate reduced fees with their [executive recruiters], which at face value make sense, but the reality is that you get what you pay for. Companies that require reduced fees from their executive search firms don't get the "A" candidates, but rather the "B" candidates. Recruiters will send their "A" candidates to the companies that pay the highest fees. Recruiters cannot afford to do as much research and "digging" for companies that require reduced fees."

Jeff H. tells clients "Don't be afraid to pay for the best, because hiring less than the best is most often the far more costly decision. A reputable recruiter saves you money by managing an efficient search and assisting you in managing the process."

How You'll Get Paid

For contingency searches, recruiters receive the entire fee once the candidate has accepted the position. For retained searches, recruiters typically receive a part of the fee once they receive the assignment, then the rest as the search continues.

Ken C., a retained recruiter, asks for 30 percent of the expected fee (because neither he nor the client knows what the salary will come out to until the candidate is hired) upon assignment, 30 percent a month later, 30 percent a month after that, and the remaining 10 percent once the candidate accepts the job. He'll adjust the remaining 10 percent to reflect the final salary, as negotiated between the client and the candidate. Manny A., who also works on retainer, asks for one-third at assignment, one-third 30 days later, and the final third 60 days later.

Tamara L., whose fee structure is a combination of retained and contingency, charges between $5,000 and $10,000 upfront, depending on the level of the search. Then her firm charges the remaining fee of 30 percent.

The one exception to the percentage rule is Vivian K. in Philadelphia, who charges an hourly rate that's capped at 30 percent of the salary. Vivian says she chose that fee structure because she was fairly new to recruiting, but she wanted to do retained searches, and clients are usually reluctant to retain recruiters with less experience. The hourly fee was a hook to attract clients.

"We were looking for a way to distinguish ourselves from other retained firms," she says. "Most executive search firms are launched by people with 20-plus years of business experience, who go on to recruit within a sector in which they have many contacts. We had none of that, so we needed a way to get our foot in the door."

Vivian says that the unusual pay structure has worked "very well in some ways and not as well in others." She says it has helped attract clients because they are willing to try her out for a few hours of work without having to commit to an entire search. On the other hand, the pay structure has made it difficult to market the firm because clients don't quite understand it. Also, she says, because other firms don't charge by the hour, clients are unsure whether she's retained or contingency. "In short," she says, "it requires a skilled marketer and business developer to make it work."

Invoice Information

Once you've filled a position, you can send an invoice, a sample of which is provided on page 191. This should be a quick description of the job completed with a calculation of the money owed. If you're working in a retained capacity, and you're asking for payment at intervals, you'll want to submit an invoice at those intervals. For example, if you want a third to start the job, a third one month later, and the final third two months later, submit an invoice at the beginning, then two more—one month and two months later. Most clients will pay you within 30 days, but keep track of when you've invoiced: If you don't receive a check a month later, call and see if there's some holdup. Every so often, an invoice is misplaced or really does get lost in the mail.

It's Taxing

Like other business owners, recruiters need to make regular payments to the IRS to avoid penalties or even a shutdown. This is true whether they operate as sole proprietors or corporations.

If you work out of your home, you can deduct part of your rent or mortgage and utilities—a big advantage to working at home. Keep in mind that you can deduct office space in your home, provided you use the space exclusively for work. If the breakfast nook is your place of business, you can't deduct it if you also use it to feed your family.

Check with an accountant before you start work as a self-employed recruiter. He or she

Smart Tip

Check out the IRS web site, www.irs.gov, for tips and tax information for small-business owners. There are FAQs, guides for starting out, and updates on the latest tax laws.

Recruiting Invoice

Placement Pals
345 Hiring Way
Job City, RI 55555

March 3, 20xx

Paul Personnel
Human Resources Manager
Wizard Widgets, Inc.
9876 Manufacturing Way
Employment, AL 44444

Invoice 2002-3

For: Filling Level I Engineer position

Amount Due: 30 percent of $85,000 annual salary, $28,333

Payment Terms: net 30 days

Rena Recruiter
Placement Pals

can help you choose a business structure and keep track of income and expenses. An accountant will also let you know what you can and can't deduct. Below are some of the expenses recruiters can deduct from their income:

- Car mileage, or other travel expenses for visiting clients or candidates
- Meals or coffee for meeting with candidates or clients
- Business calls made from a home phone
- Subscriptions to newspapers, magazines, and trade journals
- Membership in associations
- Rent
- Internet access
- Attorney's and accountant's fees
- Payments to freelance researchers or investigators
- All office supplies
- Cell phone, if it's used strictly for business

There are likely more, depending on your business. Check with your accountant.

Monthly Income and Expenses

Rena Recruiter has figured out monthly income and expenses for two possible business scenarios—the homebased one without employees, and the five-person business in a rented office space. (See Chapter 4 for initial start-up costs.)

	Homebased Business, without Employees	Five-Person Office
Monthly Expenses		
Phone	$600	$2,500
Internet connection	20	250
Web site hosting	10	150
Rent	0	2,250
Insurance for property, damage, and workers' compensation	0	575
Salaries	0	15,000
Benefits	0	4,500
Legal and accounting fees	15	250
Office supplies	20	250
Total Monthly Expenses	**$665**	**$25,725**
Gross Monthly Income	**$8,333**	**$33,333**
Net Monthly Income	**$7,668**	**$7,608**

Start-Up Expenses

Rena Recruiter is trying to decide whether to run her search firm by herself out of her home, or to open an office with a few employees. At home she already has a phone, a computer (with word processing software and internet access), and a desk, so she doesn't need to purchase those. But if she decides to start a larger business, she'll have to buy equipment for the office and for her employees. She plans to hire three recruiters and an administrative assistant. She's worked out the expenses for both scenarios:

	Solo, homebased recruiting business	Five-person recruiting firm in a rented office space
Telephones	$0	$350
Phone installation	0	250
Computers with monitors and operating systems	0	6,250
Fax machine	200	200
Copier	0	600
Printer	150	500
Desks	0	1,250
Chairs	0	500
Internet connection setup fees	0	1,500
Database software	500	1,500
Word processing software	0	100
Accounting software	0	150
Filing cabinets	50	100
Stationery	0	400
Office supplies	100	500
Business license	100	100
Market research (association membership and subscriptions)	500	500
First month of employee payroll and benefits	0	19,500
First month's rent	0	2,250
Legal fees	200	2,500
Accountant's fees	200	200
Web site design	500	500
Total	**$2,500**	**$39,700**

Staying on Top

We've covered an overview of the recruiting industry, the search process, setting up your recruiting business, and managing finances. Now it's time to wrap things up. In this chapter, we'll look at some of the ways you can keep sharpening your recruiting skills and keep your business humming along, including watching your search and place ment ratios and improving the areas where you find weak spots. We'll also give you some pearls of wisdom from our recruiters—the folks who have learned their lessons the hard way.

The Ratio

If you're having trouble getting job orders, you'll know it—your desk will be a blank slate. You'll need to hone your marketing skills. But if you're busy and you're finding that you're not pulling in as much money as you would like, it helps to look at your ratios. These will help you see if there's a problem in your search and placement process.

The ratios are the proportion of jobs moving from one stage of the process to the other—for example, the ratio of the number of people presented to the number of people hired. You can use ratios to see if there's a glitch in your process. If you find out, for example, that your ratio of candidates going from offers to acceptance is low, then you may be giving candidates unreasonable expectations about the jobs.

To figure out your proper ratios, you need to work backward. Start with your ideal annual salary: Let's say $100,000, to make things simple. Now you need to figure out how many placements you need to make to earn that salary. If you expect your average placement fee to be $20,000, that means you need to make five placements a year. If you can expect about a 75 percent offer-to-acceptance ratio in your specialty, you need to get about seven offers to achieve five placements.

Still working backward, consider how many presentations of candidates you need to achieve seven offers. If you can expect that one-third of the candidates you present will receive offers, you'll need to present 21 candidates.

Now if you actually present only about one-quarter of the candidates for whom you conduct a second interview, you'll need to conduct 84 second interviews. And if you conduct one second interview for every three first interviews that means you need 252 first interviews. Finally, if you conduct one first interview for every 20 resumes you gather, you need to compile 5,040 resumes a year! Still with us?

When you know your ideal numbers, the job is to figure out where the numbers go astray. If you're not gathering enough resumes, you need to improve your methods for finding candidates. If you're not conducting enough first interviews, you may not be selling the job well to candidates. If you're not doing enough second interviews, you may need to improve

> **Bright Idea**
>
> Check your ratios early in your career as a self-employed recruiter. Then check them every year or so to see where you've improved and where you need to keep working.

your original selection method. If you're not getting enough offers, you may need to define the job description better or you may need to prepare the candidates and clients better for the interview. Finally, if you're not achieving enough acceptances, you may be overselling the job to candidates. "If it's 12 presentations to an interview, then we're doing something wrong," says Tamara L., who runs the San Mateo, California firm.

Using ratios, you can find out where you're having trouble and correct it before you lose too much money. Unfortunately, figuring out these ratios can be a burden, and some of our recruiters admitted they haven't taken the time to do so. As Larry D. in Huntersville, North Carolina, says, "You could spend all day entering data into your computer."

Tamara L. says that her firm studies ratios, but not when they have new hires. They want to give the new recruiters time to gain some experience before they start keeping track of ratios.

If you want more information on using ratios to improve your performance, see the Appendix for Steven Finkel's book, *Breakthrough!* He includes a comprehensive section on calculating and interpreting ratios.

Placing Like a Pro

There will be a learning curve until you get into your own groove, and here are some tips to plan out your workload so that you're working like a pro:

1. *Don't try to fill every job.* Mark M. says, "Don't be too opportunistic. Save the money to support yourself so that you don't have to pursue every job offer that you have access to."
   - Successful recruiters recognize that they won't place every candidate (and shouldn't), and that they can't fill every job order.
   - Ask the client about the hiring process, how urgently they need the position filled and what happens if it isn't filled on schedule.
   - Get used to saying "no." Pros say "no" and their selectivity makes them more effective for when they say "yes."
   - Rank your job orders by letter from A to B so you can focus your efforts on those.

2. *An "A" order must have: cooperation, urgency, and marketability.*
   - Recruiting expert, Gary Stauble says that for every 15 orders that you write, maybe 5 will be worth a full search.
   - List all of your "A" deals in a prominent location.
   - Screen and prioritize your candidates too.

3. *Convey your need timeliness.*

- Let the client know that they will get a better response effort from you and your team if they are engaged in the process and provide feedback when needed.

- You need to professionally convey your expectations. Your clients will behave as you allow them.

- Explain the cases when you will require feedback or when you will be giving them updates.

- Request alerts if anything changes about the search or if they can provide any updates. Request the same from your candidates.

The "Working Smarter" Recruiter

There is a lot of work to be done and sometimes you end up putting on someone else's hat when you should be recruiting. Suddenly you're an editor, career coach, analyst and relationship expert. How do you take those hats off more often and spend more time as a recruiter?

- *Post a resume template.* Make your web site work for you. You don't need to be someone's personal resume editor, so post a few samples on your web site that they can use to customize and improve their resumes. Only they know how to fill it out, and you only recommend professional formats.

- *Create worksheets and questionnaires.* Where you might spend lots of time getting information like a researcher or reporter, you can request the same information in pre-made worksheets and questionnaires so they can be completed on the candidate's time, not yours. Do this only if you don't need to be involved.

- *Draft quick prep notes.* Some of the interview prep content is going to be the same for each candidate, so the topics that you would cover that are not job order-specific can be drafted as an attachment for them to review. For example, discussing the importance of being punctual, professional, and enthusiastic is not going to vary from candidate to candidate. Post those guidelines on your web site or e-mail them before your interview prep so that you only prep on the specific issues of that job order together.

Brainstorm more ways that you can streamline your efforts and you will find that you will have more time to dedicate to fee-earning tasks.

---

4. *Keep the lines of communication open.*
   - If you have qualified candidates and the client isn't getting back to you, let them know that you will put the search on hold until you get feedback to continue.
   - Alert them to the fact that the candidate has been responsive to their needs and timeline.
   - If you still don't get any word back, make two follow-up calls and either fax or e-mail. Don't exhaust your efforts if they remain unresponsive.

5. *Make the agreements and appointments.*
   - Book available interview times in advance.
   - List the responsibilities of the client as well as yours in the contract.
   - Schedule your next follow up call before you hang up with your client.

Fixing the Glitches

Once you discover where your weak spot lies, you'll need to work on improving it. Below are some ideas for boosting your production, wherever you need help in the process.

- Call a mentor or experienced colleague for advice.
- Reread your original training manuals.
- Ask a colleague to pretend to be a candidate or client, and give him or her your spiel over the phone. Then ask for an honest criticism. You can also record the conversation and critique it yourself.
- Make a note on your computer or your phone reminding you to make points you frequently forget.
- Study up on sales skills. Remember, recruiting is mostly a sales job.
- Re-evaluate your scripts, if you use them. If your phone-call-to-first-interview ratios are low, for example, rewrite your script for selling a position to a candidate. Try the new script out and test your ratios again.

Avoiding the Pitfalls

Our recruiters and experts agree that the most common reason for recruiting firms to fail is a lack of clients. Finding candidates for jobs is the easy part: The hard part is getting someone to pay you to do it. So recruiters need to continually drum up business, even when they're busy with job orders. Finding clients should always be the priority of the day.

Another pitfall is making a poor specialty choice. Remember, clients generally use recruiters as a last resort, so if candidates are easy to find, they're very unlikely to require your services. After all, if a client can advertise for a few hundred bucks in a trade journal and receive resumes from 20 qualified applicants, why pay a recruiter a five-figure fee? You must find a specialty in which there is a shortage of workers.

A final pitfall is trying too hard to make a match. If you send too many poorly qualified candidates to clients, your clients will stop trusting you and stop asking you to fill jobs. And they certainly won't give your name to their friends and colleagues. Our recruiters stress that you must always keep your client's priorities in mind. Do your best to understand your client's needs, and send only those candidates you sincerely believe are a good fit. Don't try to push for a match just to get a fee. It'll hurt you in the end.

Mark McConnell, one of our executive recruiting entrepreneurs drafted his Top 10 Mistakes and Advice Tips for those looking to launch their own business in the industry, which is provided on page 201.

Pearls of Wisdom

What does it take to be successful in this business? In a word: stamina. The recruiters we interviewed say the reason they've succeeded where others have failed is that they've kept at it. They keep looking for new clients and new jobs, they keep calling potential candidates, and they keep adding names to their databases.

"You have to be really focused on being successful," says Larry D. "You have to have the mentality that failure is not an option. You have to be willing to grind. You have to be willing to get on the phone and make 60 or 80 calls a day. It's hard work, especially the first year."

"There is no substitute for working the problem," agrees Vivian K., our recruiter in Philadelphia. "There's no substitute for getting in there and calling a lot of people."

We asked Mark M. his recommendations on how to have an edge in this industry. He replied, "Present a compelling value proposition to more qualified prospect companies and focus on recruiting top notch candidates that don't come from the internet job boards. You will set yourself apart. Do reference checks, degree verifications, and background checks—don't risk presenting a candidate who lied about their background."

The entrepreneurs we interviewed have learned a few more lessons along the way. The most important, they say, is to realize that much of the situation is out of their control. Clients and candidates will make their own decisions, and you can't always influence them. "I can only do as much as one person can do," says Donna K. in New York City. "I can't make somebody make an offer, and I can't make somebody take an offer."

Top 10 Mistakes and Advice for New Recruiting Businesses

1. *Write a detailed business plan!* You need to have your service offering and value proposition clearly defined, well thought out, and crafted. This business plan acts as a daily guide for business operations and decision making, as well as potentially a compelling document to help seek outside funding. The business plan keeps you focused but it's a living document you will update over time as well.

2. *Be realistic about your expenditures and revenue forecasts—start with enough money in the bank.* What are your true (not optimistic) monthly living expenses? Be brutally honest about your current lifestyle and what it costs you to live. Then don't plan on bringing in revenues for three to six months! Do you have enough capital or access to credit to survive and hit the phones without worrying about how to pay rent? Don't make the mistake of starting out under-capitalized; it can be costly later.

3. *Ask for help.* Recruiting is a team effort—don't be afraid to use contract researchers or part-time administrative help (if you can afford it). You can accomplish more in the way of research and free up more time to sell and make calls (which is where recruiters make their money)!

4. *Recruiting is a contact sport.* There is a direct correlation between the number of dials and hours spent on the phone "stirring up dust" and the amount of money you will make. This is a numbers game and he who makes the most calls wins! Some of the tools of the trade have evolved such as fax machines, the internet, and e-mail, but recruiters make money connecting with people on the phone or in person. Don't get overly dependent on electronic tools or forms of communication!

5. *Very narrowly define a niche focus—you can always expand later.* No one sees a general practitioner for brain surgery! Don't try to "just recruit anything" but select a niche that excites you and makes sense for you. Are you an industry-focused recruiting model with a nationwide territory or a functionally focused local firm? Do you focus on the "semiconductor industry" with clients and candidates across the country, or do you focus locally on a business function such as accounting or HR? One of the biggest mistakes I made was being too broadly focused. Each search you do must potentially help you either fill or acquire your next search! Build a scalable business.

6. *These days, everyone needs a web site.* Invest in a boiler-plate web site starting out. It is super cheap these days to have one made and absolutely critical if you are going to feel "real" to potential clients and candidates. It is also easy to have your hosting company track the hits to your site monthly.

Top 10 Mistakes and Advice for New Recruiting Businesses

7. *Make sure to incorporate and get the legalities out of the way*—seek the advice of a tax professional but generally as a solo S-corporation status is the best way to go. Not only will you protect your personal finances and assets, but you'll also reap the benefits if owning your own corporation. You can incorporate now for a very reasonable cost and in a short time frame using services such as the "Company Corporation." Take the time to file the necessary documents and create your company by-laws etc. If you take the time on the front end to set up your company properly and completely, you won't be distracted by this later!

8. *Stay motivated!* Figure out what your reasons are for going through the challenge of starting your own firm. Whether it is freedom, independence, the chance to help your clients and candidates, or the financial rewards from hard work, you need to find your own personal motivational triggers and remind yourself daily of why you are doing this! If you are working as a solo, staying motivated is especially difficult—listen to motivational books and tapes and surround yourself with supportive people! There are great books and tapes on the recruiting profession as well.

9. *Stay disciplined.* There will always be a hundred things to distract you from doing what you need to be doing, which is making phone calls! Block out times to make the calls (top producers make 75 plus calls a day) and execute! Reward yourself for completing these critical blocks of calls with a lunch out of the office. You MUST implement structure and disciplined action to your everyday working life. It is critical that you work really HARD especially in your first year. Block out your time, and stick to your daily plan.

10. *Don't do this unless you are 100 percent committed*—this industry takes hard work and dedication so be prepared to commit fully to making it happen even if it takes long hours and disappointing responses. You have to be 100 percent committed to being successful, and if you have the resolve to do what it takes, it is extremely rewarding.

Ken C., who works in Panama City Beach, Florida, says, "Probably the biggest mistake is overestimating your ability to control events. Sometimes you just can't put a deal together. Sometimes you just can't break through to clients."

Manny A. from Chicago adds that you can't prepare for everything. He's had some candidates accept an offer, and then drop out before the job starts. "You thought you covered all the ground ahead of time," he says, but then the candidate's family changes their mind about relocating, or a more tempting offer comes through.

Mark M. says that the hardest part about starting his own business was "realizing that just being a great recruiter is not enough. You need the other legs of the entrepreneurial barstool, including management and systems, controls and energy, and a vision. If you don't have three entrepreneurial "legs" working at the same time, you are better off getting a job at a recruiting firm where you can work on a team and have training, a draw against future commissions, marketing materials, and a phone."

Some more words of wisdom from other recruiters were:

- You can be a successful recruiter only if you truly love your job.
- Never use money as your priority when making a decision.
- People are the key in this business so network well.
- Never compromise on integrity.
- Don't let the thrill of finding the perfect "fit" fade. One person does make a difference.

Mark M. continues that his best lesson learned when starting his own business was that "I learned a great deal about business overall—it truly 'peels back the onion' of who you truly are, your determination, and your recruiting skills."

For Vivian K., the most important lesson learned is that there will always be bumps in the road. Some searches will proceed without a hitch, she says, while others will constantly trip her up. Clients will change their minds about the position requirements, candidates will drop out, or the position just isn't appealing to prospective employees.

"There's always one 'dog' search that is continuously barking," she says, "You need to take the triumphs of the day and just keep working on that dog."

Appendix
Executive Recruiting Resources

They say you can never be rich enough or thin enough. While these could be argued, we believe you can never have enough resources. Therefore, we present for your consideration a wealth of sources for you to check into, check out, and harness for your own personal information blitz.

These sources are tidbits, ideas to get you started on your research. They are by no means the only sources out there, and they should not be taken as the Ultimate Answer. We have done our research, but businesses do tend to move, change, fold, and expand. As we have repeatedly stressed, do your homework. Get out and start investigating.

Associations

American Home Business Association, 17 Harkim Road, Greenwich, CT 06831, (203) 531-8552, www.homebusiness.com

Association of Professional Recruitment Consultants (APRC), www.aprc.co.uk

American Management Association, 1601 Broadway, New York, NY 10019, (800) 262-9699, fax: (212) 903-8168, www.amanet.org

American Staffing Association, 277 South Washington Street, #200, Alexandria, VA 22314, (703) 253-2020, fax: (703) 253-2053, asa@americanstaffing.net, www.american staffing.net

National Association for the Self-Employed, P.O. Box 612067, DFW Airport, Dallas, TX 75261, (800) 232-6273, fax: (800) 551-4446, www.nase.org

National Association of Home Based Businesses, 10452 Mill Run Cir., Owings Mills, MD 21117, (410) 363-3698, www.usahomebusiness.com

National Association of Personnel Services (NAPS), P.O. Box 2128, The Village at Banner Elk, Suite 108, Banner Elk, NC 28604, (828) 898-4929, www.recruitinglife.com

National Association of Professional Employee Organizations, 901 North Pitt Street, #150, Alexandria, VA 22314, (703) 836-0466, fax: (703) 836-0976, e-mail: info@napeo.org, www.napeo.org

National Resume Writers Association, P.O. Box 475, Tuckahoe, NY 10707, (877) THE-NRWA (1-877-843-6792), www.nrwa.com

Office Business Center Association International (formerly Executive Suite Association), 15000 Commerce Parkway, Suite C, Mount Laurel, NJ 08054, (800) 237-4741, fax: (856) 439-0525, e-mail: info@officebusinesscenters.com, www.officebusinesscenters.com

Professional Association of Resume Writers, 1388 Brightwaters Blvd., N.E., St. Petersburg, FL 33704, (800) 822-7279, fax: (727) 894-1277, e-mail: PARwhq@aol.com, www.parw.com

Small Business Service Bureau, 544 Main Street, Worcester, MA 01615, (800) 343-0939, e-mail: membership@sbsb.com, www.sbsb.com

Association of Executive Search Consultants (AESC), 500 Fifth Ave., #930, New York, NY 10100, (212) 398-9556, www.aesc.org

International Association of Corporate and Professional Recruitment (IACPR), 1001 Green Bay Rd., #308, Winnetka, IL 60093, (847) 441-1644, www.iacpr.org

National Association of Executive Recruiters (for experienced, retained recruiters only), 20 North Wacker Dr., #2262, Chicago, IL 60606, (312) 701-0744

National Association of Personnel Services (for recruiters, contingency or retained, and other personnel placement types), 3133 Mount Vernon Ave., Alexandria, VA 22305, (703) 684-0180, www.napsweb.org

Note: To gain membership in associations for experienced, retained recruiters only, you have to be one of those recruiters who primarily does retained searches, which usually requires several years of experience. The typical cost of membership in a professional association is $500 or so a year.

Government Agencies

Bureau of Labor Statistics, Division of Information Services, Postal Square Building, 2 Massachusetts Avenue NE, Washington, DC 20212, www.stats.bls.gov

U.S. Census Bureau, 4700 Silver Hill Road, Suitland, MD 20746, (301) 457-4608, www.census.gov

U.S. Department of Labor, 200 Constitution Avene NW, Washington, DC 20210, (202) 693-4650, www.dol.gov

Small Business Administration, 409 Third Street SW, Washington, DC 20416, (800) 827-5722, www.sba.gov

Association of Small Business Development Centers, 8990 Burke Lake Road, Burke, VA 22015, (703) 764-9850, fax: (703) 764-1234, e-mail: info@asbdc-us.org, www.asbdc-us.org

Service Corps of Retired Executives (SCORE) National Office, 409 Third Street SW, 6th Floor, Washington, DC 20024, (800) 634-0245, www.score.org

Franchise Opportunities

Personalized Management Associates, 1950 Spectrum Circle, Suite B-310, Marietta, GA 30067, (800) 466-SUCCESS, www.pmafranchise.com

American Recruiters, 6400 North Andrews Avenue, Suite 100, Fort Lauderdale, FL 33309, (877) 576-2271, www.americanrecruiters.com

Personnel Touch Recruiting, 15 Allstate Parkway, Suite 600, Markham, ON L3R 5B4, (905) 415-5080, www.personneltouchrecruiting.com

F-O-R-T-U-N-E Personnel Consultants, JP Dusold, Manager of Franchise Sales, jpdusold@fpcnational.com, 800-886-7839, www.fpcnational.com

Books

Closing on Objections, Paul Hawkinson, Kimberly Organization, P.O. Box 31011, St. Louis, MO 63131, (314) 965-3883, www.fordyceletter.com/closingobjections.asp

Search and Placement! A Handbook for Success, Larry Nobles with Steve Finkel, Placement Marketing Group, P.O. Box 410412, St. Louis, MO 63141, (314) 991-3177, www.larrynobles.com

Placement 2000, Anthony R. Byrne, (888) 391-3384, www.pl2000.com

Breakthrough! Steven M. Finkel, P.O. Box 41008, St. Louis, MO 63141, (314) 991-3177

Business Plans Made Easy, Mark Henricks and John Riddle, Entrepreneur Press, www.smallbizbooks.com

Get Smart! 365 Tips to Boost Your Entrepreneurial IQ, Rieva Lesonsky, Entrepreneur Magazine

Start Your Own Business: The Only Start-Up Book You'll Ever Need 4th Edition, Rieva Lesonsky, Entrepreneur Press

45 Effective Ways for Hiring Smart, Pierre Mornell, Ten Speed Press

The Everything Selling Book, Marguerite Smolen, Adams Media

Interviewing and Selecting High Performers, Richard H. Beatty, John Wiley & Sons

Online Recruiting, Donna Graham, Davies-Black Publishing

Poor Richard's Internet Recruiting, Barbara Ling, Top Floor Publishing, www.topfloor.com

Selling the Invisible, Harry Beckwith, Warner Books

Shut Up & Make More Money! The Recruiter's Guide to Talking Less and Billing More, Bill Radin, Innovative Consulting

Recruiter's Almanac of Scripts, Rebuttals and Closes, Bill Radin, Innovative Consulting

Billing Power! The Recruiter's Guide to Peak Performance, Bill Radin, Innovative Consulting

The E-Myth Revisited: Why Most Small Businesses Don't Work and What to Do About It, Michael E. Gerber, Collins Publishing

Directories

The Executive Search Research Directory, Kenneth J. Cole, P.O. Box 9433, Panama City Beach, FL 32417, (850) 235-3733

The Kennedy Directory of Executive Recruiters, Kennedy Information, 1 Phoenix Mill Lane, 3rd Floor, Peterborough, NH 03458, (800) 531-0007, www.recruiterredbook.com

Standard & Poor's Corp. S&P 500 Index, Alan Miller, McGraw-Hill

Thomas Register of American Manufacturers, Thomas Publishing

Franchisors

Recruiters Directory, Recruiters Alliance, N89 W16790 Appleton Avenue, Suite 201, Menomonee Falls, WI 53051, (262) 255-7600, www.recruitersdirectory.com

Online Recruiters Directory, P.O. Box 231109, New York, NY 10023, (775) 546-9421, www.onlinerecruitersdirectory.com

Management Recruiters International, 200 Public Square, 31st Floor, Cleveland, OH 44114, (800) 875-4000, www.brilliantpeople.com

SearchFirm.com, Cluen Corporation, 7 West 22nd Street, 5th Floor, New York, NY 10010, (212) 255-6659, www.searchfirm.com

Newsletters and Publications

Executive Recruiter News, Kennedy Information, One Kennedy Plaza, Route 12 S. Fitzwilliam, NH 03447, (603) 585-3101, www.kennedyinfo.com

The Fordyce Letter, P.O. Box 31011, De Peres, MO 63131, (314) 965-3883

The Business Owner, 16 Fox Lane, Locust Valley, NY 11560, (516) 671-8100, fax: (516) 671-8099

Entrepreneur Magazine, Entrepreneur Media Inc., 2445 McCabe Way, #400, Irvine, CA 92614, (949) 261-2325, www.entrepreneur.com

Successful Recruiters

Mark McConnell, 909 Texas Street, Unit 1808, Houston, TX 77002, (713) 775-0430, mark_recruiter@hotmail.com

Jeffrey J. Hindman, The Hindman Group, Inc., 17295 Chesterfield Airport Road, Chesterfield, MO 63005, (800) 800-9220

Manny Alves, M/J/A Partners, 2 Midwest Plaza, #800, Oakbrook Terrace, IL 60181, (630) 990-0033

Ken Cole, P.O. Box 9433, Panama City Beach, FL 32417, (850) 235-3733

Larry Duke, Management Recruiters of Charlotte North, 103 Commerce Center Drive, #102, Huntersville, NC 28078, (704) 947-0660, www.mrcn.com

Donna Krasner, Conrad Cooper Associates, 355 Lexington Ave., 11th Fl., New York, NY 10017, (212) 972-2220

Tamara Lackey, New Market Partners, 477 East Ninth Ave., #102, San Mateo, CA 94402, (650) 558-0123, www.newmarketpartners.com

Web Resources

www.airsdirectory.com, a web site dedicated to training, information services, and other tools for recruiters

www.erexchange.com, electronic recruiters' exchange site

www.careerbuilder.com, a database of job seekers with opportunities to post job openings

www.monster.com, a database of resumes; you can also post positions

www.kennedyinfo.com, home of Kennedy Information, a leading research and advisory firm for the Executive Recruiting industry and the publishers of the Kennedy Directory of Executive Recruiters.

www.recruitersforum.com, a community web site for recruiters; includes listings for recruiting jobs, events, and news in the recruiting industry, and chat rooms for recruiters

www.recruiterlink.com, a business-to-business site designed to connect corporations with executive recruiters

www.therecruitinglab.com, a coaching company that supports executive recruiters and features consultant Gary Stauble

www.jobbait.com, offers executives a direct mail resume distribution service and information

www.boardnetusa.org, online registry of non-profit board and charity leaders

www.executiveagent.com, a service of Kennedy Information that allows executives to compile a list of executive search firms and customize a list to which to send their resumes

www.rileyguide.com, offers employment opportunities and job resources and recruiting information

www.execunet.com, fee-based career management and job search membership organization for executives

www.afpnet.org, Association of Fundraising Professionals

www.asaecenter.org, American Society of Association Executives (ASAE) & The Center for Association Leadership

www.nonprofitcareer.com, official site of the Nonprofit Career Network

www.ritesite.com, fee-based career-building assistance, resume-posting, and sending site

www.netshare.com, fee-based service listing confidential job leads, resume database, and career-management tools

www.executivesonly.com, fee-based site operated by recruiting experts with several membership options

www.arthurgroup.com, fee-based candidate representation company that assists executives in preparing and assessing their development to improve placement opportunities

www.aesc.org, provides articles and resources for both candidates and recruiters as well as BlueSteps, a job search source for executives

www.CEOtrak.com, a senior executive portal for news, business info, and as well as executive compensation information

www.CFO.com, this site offers articles on executive search firms and career management

www.executiveagent.com, offers a bimonthly newsletter for job hunters as well as trend-spotting

www.jobwhiz.com, articles are written by a career consultant about cold-calling, networking and more

www.experience.com, online recruiting company for specific college and member institutions

www.executiveselect.com, publishes a daily Leaders *On The Move* newsletter and *On The Hunt* newsletter that has been highly-rated

www.theladders.com, this site is for professionals earning over $100K and offers industry-specific job boards

www.6figurejobs.com, free resume database site for senior executives

www.CEOupdate.com, fee-based site publishes CEO Job Opportunities Update bimonthly

www.therecruitinglab.com, a coaching company that helps executive search firm owners and solo recruiters

Glossary

Acceptance: when the terms and start date are agreed upon between client and candidate.

Background check: making sure there are no skeletons in a candidate's closet by asking people who have worked with or know the candidate; different from checking references, as the candidate does not supply the names.

Billing: the financial amount earned that is tied to the executive recruiter's placement of a candidate.

Blockages: typically refers to places where recruiters cannot look for candidates, usually because the company is off-limits because they are or were once clients.

Boutique firm: recruiting company that focuses on narrow niches.

Calls attempted: the number of times you dial outbound irrespective of whether you speak to someone.

Calls completed: the number of conversations made.

Candidate: someone an employee may want to hire.

Candidate blockages: candidates who can't be considered for a job order because they are being utilized actively in another search.

Candidate presentations: presentation made to either clients or other recruiters where you sell your candidate to fit a job order.

Candidate referral: the name of a potential recruit obtained from another source or recruiter.

Cash in: payment received for a completed placement.

Civil and criminal record check: a check of a candidate's name against appropriate district, regional, or national criminal and civil records.

Client: an employer who is paying a recruiter to fill a position.

Client anonymity: one of the main reasons for executive recruiting. The company's identity isn't typically revealed to a candidate until they are far along in the search but instead referred to in general terms.

Cold call: a call placed to someone you don't know and for whom you haven't been given a referral.

Commission: the percentage of the quarterly sales paid to recruiters as a bonus.

Completion rate: percentage of retained searches that result in a hire with a typical rate of 60 percent.

"Con-tainer" search: a blend of contingency and retainer; a fee arrangement that involves an initiation payment and progress payments that may not be refunded, with a completion payment paid only when a placement is made.

Contingency: a method of payment in which you don't get any money until you fill a position.

Counteroffer: case where the candidate accepts an offer from the client and the current employer offers a larger sum or incentive to remain with the company.

Direct hire: placement of a candidate directly on the payroll of the client company.

Exclusive: a contract with a client in which you are the only recruiter trying to fill a position.

Feedback or follow-up: any calls made to inquire about a send-out, can be from another recruiter, client or candidate.

Guarantee period: the amount of time a recruiter guarantees the candidate will remain on the job.

Indirect hire: contacting someone not soliciting referrals, but the recruiter hopes that potential candidate recommends themselves without having to recruit directly.

KO factors: also known as Knock Out Factors that disqualify a potential client because of inappropriate statements or business factors.

Marketing calls: sales calls made to identify potential client companies to use recruiting services.

Match: process of assessing which candidates are qualified for the job order and will be selected for send-outs .

Media check: an online check to see if the candidate has been mentioned in newspapers or other media mediums in the past several years.

MPC: also known as the Most Placeable Candidate that is qualified for the position, is sincere about making a move, requires the same package as being offered, and is available for send-outs.

Noncompete clause: a contract between an employer and employee stating that after the employee leaves the employee may not compete with the employer for a certain period of time—usually one or two years.

Offer: made by the client company to a candidate with an established start date and agreed salary.

Offers rejected: different than a counter offer; offers made by client but are rejected by candidate.

Passive candidate: someone who isn't actively looking for a job but may be interested in a new position.

Placement: extension of an offer by the client, candidate accepts, and recruiter verifies and documents the agreement outlining compensation, start date, and service fee.

Placement fee: total amount charged to the client.

Present: recommending a candidate to a client.

Prime time: considered the top revenue-producing calling hours, typically thought to be 9 A.M. to 11 A.M. and 1 P.M. to 4 P.M.

Progress payments: known as one of the main differences between retainer and contingency searches; monthly payments paid by the client based on fees and out-of-pocket expenses.

Ratio: the proportion of one step in the recruiting process to another; for example, the ratio of the number of candidates contacted to the number interviewed, the ratio of first interviews to second interviews, the ratio of second interviews to presentations, and so on.

Recruit: person found through recruiter that is interested in being placed by the recruiter.

Recruiting calls: any calls made by a recruiter in an effort to find and qualify candidates.

References: the people a candidate will list for a potential employer to contact.

Researcher: someone who finds names of candidates and often screens them on behalf of a recruiter; may be hired as a freelance worker or an employee.

Retainer: a method of payment in which the client retains a recruiter exclusively to fill a position and pays money upfront to do so.

Script: a written statement some recruiters refer to when cold calling clients or approaching candidates.

Search research: the business of finding names of possible candidates in companies similar to the client company.

Send-outs: meetings arranged by the recruiter between a candidate and a client that occurs.

Send-out arranged: same as send-outs in that they were planned but did not actually occur.

Senior executive: anyone earning more than $100,000 a year.

Service/fee agreement: verbal agreement, later documented, made by the client agreeing on payment terms, guarantee, fee formula, and terms of referral.

Source/resource: person who can suggest possible candidates to a recruiter for a search.

Source company: a company that is not a client and therefore may be a source of candidates.

Super-executive: a manager who combines the abilities and experience of the two or more people they are replacing.

Suspect: a person that could become a possible candidate for a search assignment but has yet to be interviewed or screened.

Work a desk: doing the job of finding clients and recruiting candidates, as opposed to managing other recruiters.

Index

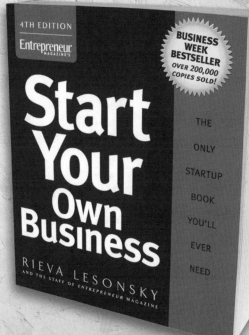

10/25/07